F$C-K YOU MONEY

A MIND-BLOWING MINDSET CHANGE INTO
A FUTURE OF CONTENTED INDEPENDENCE

by

BOBBY RAKHIT

F$CK YOU MONEY

ISBN: 978-1-7391974-2-1 (paperback)
ISBN: 978-1-7391974-1-4 (hardcover)
ISBN: 978-1-7391974-0-7 (ebook)

Interior Layout: Ravi Ramgati

fkyoumoney.org

For Rohit and Maya

Rohit and Maya, I dedicate this book to you because you matter to me and influence my life, which is enough to fill another book.

The age-old tradition of authors dedicating books to people stems from the need to acknowledge their influence on the writing of the book, their childhood, their education, their career, and their lives. Writing a book and releasing it is like kicking a young bird out of the nest to let it find its wings and fly. Survival depends on the self-confidence the bird achieves with its first successful flight, no different to sending a child into the world to find their way, to test their wings and soar.

As I invite my readers to explore new ideas about living a life of well-being, I encourage you to be inquisitive. Don't simply accept what you hear or see. Question the truth of it. As your world enlarges, don't stop looking for answers to your questions. The universe is yours to explore. The only thing to take out of the past is wisdom. Use it to mix with the intellect of your young minds, constantly shaping your future.

It's yours to change.

There has never been a more exciting time to be alive, a maxim that will ring true each day as you pursue purpose and meaning in your lives.

The Rakhit Foundation

Beneficiaries

The Rakhit Foundation is the fulfilment of a non-profit enterprise's dream to launch upliftment projects. The initial project will focus on selecting a small group of young orphans in Africa to assist with their daily needs, health, and education. The proceeds of the book sales, including the rest of the series, will go towards this and future projects. Online customers purchasing any version of the book (paperback, eBook, or audio) can donate one or more copies of any selected version through the website at www.fkyoumoney.org.

Table of Contents

Introduction

Hi, I am Bobby Rakhit, the creator of 'F$CK YOU MONEY' (FuM©), a somewhat unusual title for which I make no excuse; if you want to understand the concept, read the book. Whether this is the first or last business book you read, you *will* gain new insights and experience a few epiphanies by the time you reach the final page. I have written the *contents* of this book to shock you more than the title does, introducing you to an entirely new paradigm. Insights and ideas about the business of doing life. Doing life *well*, right through to its end. It is the first in a series of books that will turn your thinking inside-out, upside-down, and back to front. Changing your established mindsets to take you to a destination far from the one to which you are currently headed.

Think life on another planet.

I am interested in anyone who is ready for an adventure. If you are between twenty-five to thirty-five years old living in *extended adolescence*, I am talking to you. If you're unemployed, binge-watching TV series on Mom and Dad's couch, living in an unrealistic bubble of carefree juvenescence, I am talking to you. If you're drifting on the wind of chance, hoping it will somehow get you where you want to be, I am talking to you. And anyone else between the age of student and pensioner.

The industrial revolution birthed new careers far from the previous regime of family enterprises. The days when farmers, village cobblers, and blacksmiths were introduced to mechanised systems, creating jobs to suit the evolving progress of human needs. It was an unstoppable

process of rapid development. Nothing compared to the lightning-fast digital revolution we live in right now, at a pace we hope to hold on to by our fingertips. The sweet spot of living life contentedly between fulfilled job satisfaction and a balanced personal life has become an elusive dream.

For most, it is more of a work-life *imbalance*.

Perfecting the way to say 'F$CK YOU MONEY' is learning to massage a successful career into a sustainable future of meaningful, satisfied contentment.

Welcome aboard.

I guarantee you an exciting journey.

Your FuM© Director,

Bobby Rakhit
Entrepreneur, Author,
Philanthropist, Creator of FuM©

Prelude

Survival – A Story of Man's Evolution

BANG!

It took 13.47 billion years until the Mesozoic era began 230 million years ago. When tyrannosaurus rex and the long-necked brontosaurus roamed the rugged earth, the terrifying pterosaurs ruled the skies preying on fish and other small animals. Survival was an ongoing challenge in what looks like a violent 186 million years on earth. This 66-million-year era finally ended with an incident that even the fittest couldn't survive, and they all eventually starved to death.

FF 2.5 million years

What are the chances?

The world lay fallow until between five and seven million years ago when our ancestors arrived in the form of apelike creatures who walked on their two hind legs. Another two to three million years passed before they evolved into the beginning of the Palaeolithic Period, about 2.5 million years ago. These humans lived in caves, huts, and tepees, hunting and gathering to sustain themselves. They were around until the aftermath of an exploding comet sent a mass of fireballs raining down on the earth. This was the beginning of their progressive demise until the last caveman died a lonely death, ending his fight for survival.

Unbelievable!

The Earth just happens to be in a universe we still have not found the end of. Think about it; There are ten known dimensions, and scientists suspect an eleventh exists. Nine dimensions of space and one of time. And *we exist in this*! Absolutely incredible! Talk about insignificance. Just stand next to an ant and try to get a perspective from its position.

Δ PLAY

SURVIVAL – THROUGH ADVERSITY, COURAGE, AND PROSPERITY

Meet Nogg, a rather hairy, smelly caveman. He has a woman, and she is pregnant with their first cave child. Life has been hard for Nogg, and it shows. His leathery, cracked, sun-baked hide and missing finger and toenails bear testimony to this fact. Simple survival has been a daily grind against the harsh elements, wild animals, and marauding clans, and now his nagging woman has a belly as big as a rock. Just one more frustration in Nogg's trying caveman existence.

He was orphaned as a very young caveboy when the rest of his family was wiped out. He was no higher than three Compsognathus (a chicken-sized carnivorous dinosaur) when a forest fire wiped them out as they foraged for nuts and berries. He would have been fossilised ash if not for his aching gut keeping him confined to their cave on that ill-fated day. His nomadic family was rejected by their clan because of his father's deformed leg. A deformity that forced him to fend for himself from an early age by foraging for berries and the odd bit of seasonal fruit. He moved far away from the clan's territory to avoid the brutal backlash toward him. Finding a woman to procreate with when he reached puberty was a colossal challenge—one he pursued as aggressively as searching for food. A challenge that luckily for Nogg ended in success one day when his father bumped into Nogg's mother. She was as bedraggled as him and had been evicted from *her* clan for her gammy right hand.

It was love at first sight.

Life was tough for a vegetarian family with changing seasons producing limited supplies forcing them into a nomadic cycle of finding a cave near a source of food and water. The scarcity of nutritious food produced sickly, skinny little kids just like their parents. It was a miracle that none of them carried deformities of any kind, but it never meant their attempts at hunting were any more successful than their father's. They did manage on the odd occasion to bag a rock rabbit with less flesh than bones. By the time the fire took Nogg's family out, they had covered thousands of miles over rough country chasing food far away from their original clans. Poor little Nogg according to strict clan lore had no chance of reconnecting with them even if he found his way back to his parents' clans of origin. He searched desperately to find a friendly clan to take him in.

His survival hung in the balance between trying to fend for himself or follow the lure of clan food at the risk of death by human hands sooner than starvation. Fortunately for him, cave dwellers were not cannibalistic. Besides, the lack of flesh on his skinny bones did not offer more than a mouthful for a hungry caveman.

Fortune favours the brave (AKA desperation)

Picture the scene—a skinny kid appears out of the bush in the path of a group of well-fed young adolescent cave-teens out on a hunt. He bravely stands his ground, rubbing his hollow stomach with one hand, screwing his face up tight and tapping the tips of his five fingers against his lips with the other, showing his plight. Not that his skeletonised condition doesn't make his predicament glaringly obvious.

After several attempts, retreating back into the bush and reappearing, narrowly escaping the flying rocks and verbal abuse hurled at him, one young hunter steps in and saves his hide. *Aux* is different from the rest of the gang. He commands the gang to stop, facing them off with Nogg cowering behind him. Aux is as big as a cave bear but gentle as a rock dove. He is not like anyone Nogg has ever known. At first, Nogg is suspicious of his kindness, expecting Aux to turn on him in a flash as his siblings did. He can not believe that somebody other than his mother is being gentle towards him. Especially someone who could end his life with a swift slap. Aux takes him by the hand, inviting him into the hunting party. A very successful hunt it turns out to be, too. They bag a few bush pigs and several wild hares, creating the sweetest memory of Nogg's first real hunt.

Back with the clan, the smell of fresh meat is enough to drive his hunger wild. He has to hold himself back from climbing on the fire to rip hot meat off the roasting bush-pig. When he finally sinks his teeth into a juicy piece, his gut lets him know it is not used to processing anything other than berries and nuts and tiny bits of raw rock rabbit. But it only takes a few days for it to adjust.

Nogg's introduction to Aux's family is not as pleasant as meeting Aux alone. The responses vary, from the father, who is not pleased to have an extra mouth to feed to Aux's mother, who shares her son's gentleness. His father immediately increases Aux's daily list of domestic chores and bumps up his hunting quota. Aux's seven sisters and three brothers, of which Aux is the eldest, cackle and poke him in his scrawny ribs. They have never been as malnourished as him, even in the worst droughts. Aux agrees to all the extra work, taking on the sole responsibility of caring for Nogg. He goes so far as to let Nogg share his bed until he can secure a bearskin for him. The nourishing new diet soon puts some meat on Nogg's bones and gives him the strength to chip in and help Aux with his chores. The 'terrible ten' stop poking him in the ribs and lose interest in teasing him.

→ **FF** Teenage cave boy

By the time he is five Compsognathus high, Nogg has grown into a large, muscular, self-assured hunter, thanks to Aux's patient tutelage. The father is less angry with him now that he is earning his keep with daily additions to the dinner pot. Often hunting alone, Nogg enjoys the solitude of the forest without a noisy bunch of mates chasing the prey away. He's learned to fit in by mimicking Aux's behaviour and even made friends with some of his peers.

Aux's eldest sister Zugg takes a shine to Nogg, and he often catches her staring at him and blushing bright red when he spots her. He struggles to make sense of the fuzzy feelings rippling through his gut every time it happens.

When he isn't hunting or being admired by Zugg, Nogg is at his favourite spot in the river splashing the ice-cold water over his grubby body. It is on one of these lazy days while having a dip that he has a close encounter with a Megalania (an alligator-like creature with huge teeth) that could easily end his life or at least rip off a limb. Sitting quietly in the shallows, he hears a ripple in the reeds behind him. The mayhem of splashes and blurred movement suddenly end with the loud clap of its closing jaws, fortunately for Nogg not followed by excruciating pain. When he sees its mouth opening again within striking distance of his right leg, about to lunge, he instinctively pulls back out of its reach. The razor-sharp teeth in its open jaws give him the wings he needs to lift his dripping wet body out of the water and plant his feet safely on a dry rock. Then one more jump and he is satisfyingly far enough to watch the predator's forlorn retreat. His heart thumps so loudly in his chest that it feels like it will burst. It takes a few minutes for his breathing to slow down to a comfortable rhythm. Letting rip with a bone-shaking "HAAAGGHHH!!" he picks up his wooden spear and waves it at the Megalania's long tail. This is not to be the last close encounter with wild animals for Nogg. Collectively, the incidents hone his impressive lightning-quick reflexes to life-saving perfection.

→FF Young adulthood (AKA testosterone overload)

Zugg's sneaky stares turn into bold flirting and shy smiles, which are instinctively acknowledged and returned with boyish charm. It isn't long before the two young lovebirds make their feelings for each other public. When Nogg finally understands the fuzzy feelings, he plucks up the courage to ask for her hand and the rest of her luscious body. Zugg's father is just too pleased to get rid of the two of them and makes sure they move far away to make their new life. He's made no secret of his intense dislike of Nogg, and now he is glad to see their departing footprints in the dust outside his cave.

Bundling up their meagre belongings, they set off on their 'honeymoon' to find a suitable cave. Nogg is sad to leave Aux but is sure their paths will cross again in the future.

→→ FF Marital bliss

The sun is just making its appearance on the distant horizon. Nogg is standing on a rock outside his cave with his hands cupped around his mouth. Bellowing at the top of his gruff voice, he broadcasts his dominant presence. His warning to the waking world. *Don't mess with me*!

"Eeeoweeeee, eeeowoooo, eeeoweeee, eeeowoooooooooo!!!"

Waving his heavy wooden spear defiantly, he takes a deep breath, beats his chest with his free hand, and repeats the warning.

"Eeeoweeeee, eeeowoooo, eeeoweeee, eeeowoooooooooo!!!"

Anybody or anything in the vicinity will be aware of the consequences of entering his realm uninvited. The bellowing goes on for what seems to Zugg like a zillion years as she lies irritated and cold, trying to get a few more minutes' sleep. Pulling the thick furry cavebear skin up over her head, she tries to drown out the noise and keep the cold air off her shivering body. Stomping back inside, Nogg leaves his thundering bellows disappearing in the distance, echoing the defiant warning. Throwing his spear onto the pile of weapons in the back of the cave, he walks over to the smouldering fire, pokes it with a log, and bending low, blows hard into the dying coals to tease out some warmth.

Sticking her head out from under the covers, Zugg grunts angrily at him, showing her displeasure. Unperturbed, Nogg waves his big hairy arm dismissively at her. Rummaging around the fire looking for something to eat, he grunts loudly, giving up in despair when he finds nothing. Zugg pulls the skin closer and sits up, her big bare breasts resting on her pregnant belly. Looking straight at him, she raises her shoulders and eyebrows as if to say, *Where the hell should I get food?* Shaking his head in desperation, Nogg taps his thick lips with puckered fingertips, rubbing his empty belly like he did the first time he met Aux. Raising her shoulders again, Zugg stretches out her arms with empty palms turned skyward. The atmosphere in the cave is grim after days without food and very little water. The river that flowed so strongly when they arrived is now a muddy puddle. The regular animal spoor has disappeared like the drops of water on the sun-baked ground. Nogg and Zugg's hunger and thirst get more wretched with each distressingly dry breath.

He has failed to bag an animal or found any berries for many long days. His bellowing and chest-thumping haven't brought any neighbouring clans to his cave thinking he might be protecting a food supply either. They must have no food as well or have moved away in search of some. The fact that he is a great hunter and a fierce protector of his wife and home doesn't make up for the lack of food in their cave. Zugg's hunger intensifies by the second as her depleted body tries to feed the child growing inside her. She hates Nogg for the state she is in, carrying his child that is slowly sapping her life away. In desperation, she wishes she was back home with her parents, where she is sure they have tons of food.

Nogg's preoccupation with *his* hunger and the frustration of long days on failed hunts is getting to *him* too. Sitting in the blistering sun next to the muddy puddle of a river day after day, waiting for raindrops or anything edible to appear has driven him to think—an activity that doesn't come naturally to his tiny brain. It is time to move and move quickly, but Zugg is in no condition to take a long hike over rocks and mountains in the hope of finding something to eat and water to drink. He has to find food and bring it to her or take her to it. He is as desperate as the skinny orphan who bumped into Aux and his mates all those years ago.

Zugg waves him angrily out of the cave, rubbing her belly, and tapping *her* puckered fingers painfully against her hungry lips, grimacing and grunting loudly.

"Ghaaaghh, ghaaaghh, ghaaaghh."

Nogg responds angrily. Waving his big, hairy arm dismissively at her again, he turns away, hiding his shame and avoiding her glaring eyes. Picking up a spear, he flicks his head defiantly back at her, exiting the cave and growling loudly.

"Haaagghhh!"

It is the last sound she will hear for a few days as she crawls back under the warm bearskin. Letting out a long, hungry sigh, she manages to fall into a welcome state of slumber. Thoughts of the new life inside her have occupied her mind each waking minute of the day. She is sure it is another Nogg, strong as a cavebear with as much hair covering his body. She pictures him playing and fighting like her brothers did growing up. The hunger cramps raging in her empty stomach wake her with dread in the quiet cold cave. Hoping against hope that Nogg will bring something home for the pot, she falls back into a delirious haze of anguished sleep tormented by dreams of her baby dying of starvation inside her.

Her faculties eventually begin to vacillate in and out of a state of delirium. Hallucinations take her to her family after a day's bountiful hunting and berry gathering. She is eating through mountains of delicious roasted venison and munching handfuls of brightly coloured berries chased down with what feels like a river of water. The scene suddenly changes, and she is sobbing uncontrollably back in the quiet cave starving to death. She begins to cackle as she sees her ten siblings as scrawny as Nogg the first day she met him. The next scene appears with her feeling a warm, calm glow come over her whole body as she lies safely in Nogg's hairy arms.

Scene after scene play havoc with her unconscious mind, driving her close to the edge of insanity. She tries desperately to wake up and escape the horrors, sobbing, laughing, smiling, cackling, and sobbing, again and again...

→→**FF** Three days later

Through the haze of her delirium, Zugg hears a familiar noise. Nogg is bellowing in the distance. Faint and far off, the familiar sound is getting louder and louder.

"Eeeoweeeee, eeeowoooo, eeeoweeee, eeeowoooooooooo!!!"

"Eeeoweeeee, eeeowoooo, eeeoweeee, eeeowoooooooooo!!!"

"Eeeoweeeee, eeeowoooo, eeeoweeee, eeeowoooooooooo!!!"

Is her mind still playing tricks on her? She feels big strong hairy arms cradling her head and cool water trickling past her cracked lips down her parched throat. She has been here too many times in the last few days to believe it is true. Then the smell of Nogg's dusty skin triggers life into her depleted body. Forcing her dry eyes open, she emerges from the hell of her delirium as the blurry vision of her husband slowly clears into focus. The dead rock rabbit he is holding up by the ears sends saliva drooling from her gaping mouth.

It *isn't* another cruel hallucination!

ΔII PAUSE

Two days of hard running, boulder-hopping, and tree climbing to survey the lie of the land through virgin forests and arid plains and crawling through dense bush have ended with Nogg perched on the edge of a cliff. Breathless and exhausted, he stands open-mouthed, taking in a view that injects a lightning bolt of energy through his tired body. When his gaze finally drops to his bleeding feet, he sees fresh animal spoor in the sand. The pain in his legs suddenly lifts; there is food around. After two lonely days of silence, other than his heavy breathing, the unfamiliar sound of crashing water is deafening. Nogg's high perch is next to something he is seeing for the first time in his life: tons of water crashing over rocks and cascading into a river far below. The excitement, fear, and confusion are almost too much for his tiny brain to cope with. The loud pounding of his heart pulsing in his head doesn't help clear the fog. The cool spray of water on his face dribbles into his mouth, breaking his long thirst and clearing his mind. He sees a herd of buck drinking in the river below and trees with branches bending under the weight of the fruit they bear.

He has stepped out of a dream into paradise.

Δ PLAY

Nogg, Zugg, and Dudd, a very large baby boy, have relocated and are happy to be living in a new cave close to the rushing river below the roaring waterfall. Dudd was born the night Nogg returned home. They couldn't wait to get out of their old cave to the paradise Nogg found. He carried his boy in a bearskin pouch on his back, while Zugg, whose belly was somewhat smaller, walked comfortably all the way to their new home.

Nogg is sitting comfortably on a rock outside his new cave taking in the beauty surrounding him and enjoying the fact that his family is safely taken care of. He spots something grazing in the distance and thinks back to the two days of hell that brought him here. He never wants to be in the same predicament ever again. Boyhood memories of his family's continuous struggles for survival have always haunted him. They were always moving to new caves when the food ran out or a drought hit only because they'd never considered the future as they greedily raped the supply before simply moving on.

He remembers a lesson he learned from Aux hunting with the rowdy gang one hot summer day. Aux tried unsuccessfully to stop them when they came across some easy pickings and went wild killing more animals than they needed. Half of that day's bag was thrown into a pit to rot, much to Aux's horror. He told Nogg to always think of the future and never take more than he needed, explaining that the animals needed to breed and produce more young. Aux showed him to always select females for the pot and spare the males because they were in the minority.

The day he stood at the top of the cliff looking at the herd of buck in the distance was the day he decided to follow that wisdom and manage his hunting to conserve the supply. He would never do another desperate run to find food again. The plan included the expansion of cultivating crops fruit, nuts, and veggies too. He wished he could preserve the meat for the lean times (very advanced thinking for a caveman). Instead, he built a small dam to save water to get him through the next drought and keep the animals watered.

Genius thinking for the times! (the beginning of Nogg's FuM©)

ΔII **PAUSE** A very sad side story

Nogg put his pride in his pocket when they were dying of hunger and buried the memory of how Zugg's father had evicted them from his

cave. He went back to ask for help. The horrific scene he was met with shook him to the core. The stench of rotting flesh hit his nose before the sight of the scattered dead bodies. There was no sign of life anywhere; the caves were all empty. Examining each decomposing body, he found Zugg's whole family, except for Aux. By the looks of it, they had starved to death. There was no leftover food lying around as there usually was. It was just like them to be too stubborn to move on or ask for help. Aux had probably moved off on his own and had hopefully found food and water.

Δ **PLAY**

Zugg emerges from the cave carrying Dudd on her hip. Nogg's interrupted thoughts turn to Dudd's future and how he can help him avoid the mistakes *he* has made. Dudd's life *will* be different. With his limited vocabulary unable to verbalise the love he feels for his boy, he lets his actions speak instead and wraps the pair of them in a tight bear hug, telling Zugg that he will always be there for her and their boy.

FF Dudd, the teenager

Dudd has grown into a strong young fellow just over six Compsognathus high, well nourished by abundant good food and a lot of exercise helping his father hunt and tend the crops. He has siblings: two brothers and a sister. When he was only three Compsognathus high, Nogg noticed Dudd's curiosity around the fruit trees and berry bushes, digging around the stems looking at the roots.

ΔII **PAUSE** A backstory from Nogg's memory

Nogg's father had tried his hand at growing food by planting nuts in the ground after accidentally uprooting a small tree and finding a seed with the shoot growing out of it. What he never did, though, was to water it. This was another lesson Nogg learned from Aux.

Δ PLAY

He began teaching Dudd how to plant seeds and tend to them. Some grew, some didn't, but the boy persisted and developed into a prodigious farmer. Needing some independence, Dudd moved out of Noggville into his own cave not far away from the family. He set himself up with a grove of nut trees, berry bushes, and veggies. Being an enterprising young man, he became a better hunter than Nogg and even taught himself to carve things out of wood with sharp rock tools.

→→FF Dudd, the young adult

His hormones are driving him nuts. He consults Nogg to find out what he should do. He ventures out on a perilous quest to find a woman. Cresting a hill, he drops to his knees when he sees movement in the valley. Four young girls are bathing in a river. Crouching low, he makes his way down the slope to a clump of trees and climbs one to get a good view. Instinctively selecting a favourite as if he is hunting a bush pig, he doesn't take his eyes off her. Her long dark hair and curves in the right places drive his hormones wild. He bites his lip hard to avoid calling out to her. To make matters worse, the girls come out of the water and lie on the rocks, their wet bodies baking in the late afternoon sunshine.

When the sun drops behind the hills, they slip into their bearskin skirts and disappear up a well-worn path. Dudd lets out a desperate sigh so loud that his dark-haired beauty stops in her tracks to look back at what made the noise. Squinting in the fading light, she cannot see him in the tree. Her curiosity gets the better of her, and she ventures towards him. His heart rate threatening to explode, his sweaty hands nearly lose their grip on the branches.

"Haaagghhh! Haaagghhh!"

A loud roar comes from higher up the path. A monster of a man comes into view; grabbing the young girl roughly by the arm, he drags her back

up the path, grunting loudly. Assuming it is her father, Dudd's hopes of ever seeing her again sink in despair.

→→FF A happy couple

Jegg, the beauty with long dark hair and curves that drove him wild, is happily settled with him in Duddville. She bore Dudd Junior, a healthy bouncing boy, on the precise day of the average gestation period of a cave baby from the day they eloped from Jegg's clan.

Her curiosity took her back the next day to where she had heard the loud sigh coming from the bushes. Finding Dudd's footprints under the tree, she looked up to where he had spent the night. Their eyes met—love at first sight. Almost falling out of the tree in a rush, he grabbed her hand, and they never stopped running until they got to Duddville.

ΔII **PAUSE** Desperate neighbours

Nogg and Zugg are sound asleep on a cold winter morning in Noggville. Zugg wakes to a croaking noise outside the cave. Listening carefully, she hears a cough. She digs her elbow into Nogg's ribs and motions for him to get his spear and see who is outside. Up in a flash, spear in hand, ready to protect his realm, he rushes out of the cave stark naked.

His adrenalin stops pumping at the sight of the skin-and-bones bedraggled teenager snivelling behind a rock. Unsure whether the kid is a decoy, he grabs him by the throat, threatening to drive his spear through the boy's heart. When he is satisfied there is no threat, he pulls the spear back and lets him go. It turns out that his family clan was attacked, leaving most of the men dead, the women dragged off, and all of their belongings plundered. His younger siblings and mother hid in a secret part of their cave, and he was severely beaten and left for dead.

Flashback!

Nogg remembers when Aux took him by the hand, defying his peers, and showered him with love and kindness.

Δ **PLAY**

Nogg gets his boys together, packs some food, a few cavebear skins and some water, and they set off with the boy. When they get there, Nogg sees things that tell him these people were craftsmen, more skilled than Dudd. The mother and siblings are reluctant to leave their hiding place until the boy reassures them that Nogg and his sons are friendly. The sight of food and water is enough to defeat their fear.

→→**FF** Good neighbours

An interdependent relationship grows from that day and turns into a flourishing partnership. The families share the proceeds of each other's skills and produce. Nogg trades his food bounty for the neighbour's fancy implements. The Noggs and Dudds came to grips with using spoons and cooking on hot rocks. Zugg loves using the pestle and mortar to crush seeds and grain. The neighbours grow fat and healthy on their consistent food supply.

EVOLUTION

Nogg's hard work and discipline eventually created his sustainable state of 'F$CK YOU MONEY!' (FuM©). The recurring flow of food and water along with practical utensils meant he was independently content. He laid the FuM© foundation, leaving a legacy that changed his clan's future. His influence spread to many neighbours, saving them from a struggling existence. He spent his latter days doing exactly what he wanted to do, when he wanted to, and turned down any offers of increasing his sufficient bounty saying:

"Haaagghhh!" (AKA F$CK YOU MONEY!)

At least, until the comet sent fireballs raining down on earth to end his existence.

→→FF A few million years

Modern humans, Homo sapiens, evolved from the previous Homo erectus humans who lived between 1.9 and 1.35 million years ago. It is hard to believe that our species has been around for 200,000 years and they were the first to be labelled 'wise man' ('sapiens' in Latin). We live in a period where evolution has taken on supersonic speed compared to the previous ages, and it doesn't look like it will be slowing down anytime soon either. The history of our evolution is magnificently written into the genome, the set of genetic instructions containing all of the information needed to build Homo sapiens, packaged into 23 pairs of chromosomes.

We *are* amazing creatures.

F$CK You Money (FuM©) – FuM© 101

Isn't music amazing? Millions of tunes are composed from a base of just seven notes: C, D, E, F, G, A, and B that make up a octave. Played haphazardly, they sound awful. But in the hands of a trained musician, they become as easy as learning *do, re, mi, fa, sol, la, ti* from the famous movie *Sound of Music* from the '60s. It opened a new understanding for the unschooled musical public by hearing the sound of the notes.

I'm by no means a musician, but I *am* creative, and the three basic letters I used to write my tune and simplify the understanding of a brand-new culture are F, U, and M. This culture will revolutionise the way discerning individuals live contented, productive, and meaningful lives. FuM©'s three simple letters can be blended into millions of melodies to suit any individual choosing to predict their future as opposed to leaving it up to a faceless system to provide. Unlike music, FuM© **is** *all* inclusive and needs only your commitment to pen the melody.

It's not clear at what point Nogg was around in the evolution of cavemen, but what is clear is that he improved the lives of his family and the rest of the species that caught the vision. He took them out of the nomadic rut they were stuck in.

As smart as we are today, nothing has changed. We're caught in a rut just like the cavemen were. There were small tweaks to the Palaeolithic system, like Aux's clan, who found better ways to hunt, gather, and store food without refrigerators. Discovering fire and making implements from rocks, wood, and twine were massively progressive advances.

→→FF The present

We might develop at the speed of light today, but human well-being is steadily regressing. Mental illness has never been as prevalent as it is today. Depression, surprisingly, was first diagnosed as recently as 1930, giving it a label. Today the World Health Organisation estimates that 3.8 percent of the 7.9 billion Homo sapiens walking the planet are coping with depression. That is a whopping 303.2 million people! That's an evolutionary statistic we cannot be proud of. Depressed people make up a number close to the population of the US. We work hard at treating the symptoms but fail dismally at treating the cause.

When it comes to managing our finances, the pace of evolution is largely stuck on a 'rinse and repeat' conveyer belt with minor changes introduced out of necessity rather than radical innovation. Another worrying fact is that a large percentage of the 303.2 million depressed souls are struggling with financial issues.

It's time to treat this stagnation with a combination of F, U, and M to restore mental well-being and introduce practical individual financial management for everyone. I am not throwing the baby out with the bathwater, but I want to shake things up for the baby to feel uncomfortable enough to hold on and wait for it to be replaced with *fresh* warm water.

This is where the culture of FuM©**'s practical approach to creat**ing a future life of well-being begins.

F$CK YOU MONEY is a culture that exists between the ancient wisdom of deep thinkers and modern capitalism. Not Socrates and Plato from 347 BC, I'm talking about 300 years earlier when Buddha the teacher, philosopher, and spiritual leader was around and essentially teaching us that the ego must be dethroned from the misconception that it is an entity that exists by itself. Once we do this, we can have an authentic relationship with our true selves. Buddhism teaches us to put our ego in its rightful place as an advisor, not as our identity, and to have freedom from our conditioned thinking. Once you do this, you will be a happier person. When you free your mind from a static identity, then you are open to change and external circumstances. Fundamentally, as with most ancient wisdom, it teaches the basic precept of equality and reciprocity amongst our fellow humans. Biblical truth tells us we are all created equal and should do unto others as we would have them do unto us. Embracing this truth and posture, you will find yourself flowing naturally into the disciplines of practicing concentration, meditation, and mental development to gain insight, wisdom, enlightenment, and well-being.

If you combine this mindset with the worldly system of capitalism, understanding that the intrinsic value of money is finite, you will find yourself living in the culture of FuM©.

A significant piece of the FuM© puzzle formed in my mind many years ago when visiting the Egyptian pyramids, I saw the foolishness of placing eternal worth on the intrinsic finite value of money and objects. The pharaohs had been mummified and laid to rest in ornately decorated caskets, surrounded with chairs and tables, jewels and trinkets to use in the *afterlife*. I only knew this because our guide told us. By the time we stood in the tombs, they were totally empty. The valuables, including the mummified body, had been removed by raiders.

The bottom line:
There is no question that we need money to survive in a capitalist society.

The question:
Are you ready to change your thinking to evolve with the ancient wisdom that promises an independent life of well-being?

FuM© is a flexible discipline that needs to be monitored as opposed to micro-managed with the mindset that the only constant in the process, as in life, is change. Once my FuM© goals were set, I progressively adjusted my compass as the goalposts shifted.

"Goalposts?" you ask.

Circumstances changed within my businesses, my family, and the world (COVID-19 pandemic), and my aged grandmother came to live with us, all in the space of three years.

I like to read autobiographies; I have even written my own for my family to read. There are no identical autobiographies. Some parts may be similar but never identical. Life stories are made up like the facets of a diamond. No two diamonds are identical, yet they are complete and uniquely beautiful. Writing the FuM© melody for your life is the same as cutting a diamond: The tune will change to fit the lyrics. You wouldn't expect a coal miner to cut a rough diamond into shape, so pay careful attention to how you plan your FuM©. It is not a haphazard *wait-and-see* process. Your achievement depends on good mentors, intentionally educating yourself, and acquiring the new skills and knowledge you need.

You cannot become a car by sleeping in a garage.

The following simple example explains a critical facet to ensure you enjoy long-term meaningful FuM©.

The Grant study, which I will cover in more detail, makes the point that good relationships produce a successful life, to which I add, a good-looking FuM©. Besides having mentors, gaining knowledge through education, applying your creativity, and so on, solid relationships with people close to you provide support and keep you on track.

You will no doubt have to explain FuM© to the people close to you and keep them informed of your progress. Don't be surprised when you experience pushback and find yourself isolated, feeling lonely, or questioning your decision. Because there is a strong possibility that they just *don't get it*. Be patient and gentle with them. FuM© is a unique idea, although hopefully not for long now that this book is spreading the concept. Recall the ancient wisdom about your ego wrapped up in pride and wanting to be stroked.

But that's not the authentic you.

I keep regular contact with close friends, who are aware of and share my FuM© vision. This is a select few that are like the siblings I never had. In this band of brothers, we speak freely into each other's lives without needing permission. We trust each other enough to accept any comments or at least debate difficult topics that come up. This inner circle supports me through the unpredictable rapids in the river of my life. The circle is spread across continents, making regular one-on-one contact difficult. Nonetheless, we keep contact, hold each other accountable, and support the other members' dreams and aspirations.

Follow the Grant study's advice and don't neglect to build a tight network of trusted connections that can undergird you when life gets difficult. If you don't, you will wish you had when the time comes.

The next question:

What exactly has the capitalistic order and a status quo mindset done for us?

Ask Joe Bloggs, seventy-two, looking more like ninety-two, living in a retirement home knitting bed socks to supplement his income more than the need to pass the time and kill the boredom of long, empty days.

When Joe was in his thirties, he was promised an amazing retirement with regular vacations on exotic islands. He would have enough money to buy a house on the beach and eat meals in fancy restaurants. He could buy the car of his dreams and play golf three times a week. To date, Joe has knitted away several hundred miles of sheep's wool. He lives in a state-run retirement home with three meals a day that he is sick of eating and a bunch of grumpy old people.

Who promised Joe *the life of Really*?

The person who sold him the retirement dream he paid into religiously every month for forty-five years. *And* the lyrics of the popular 1880s song.

Is that Mr. Reilly, can anyone tell?
Is that Mr. Reilly that owns the hotel?
Well, if that's Mr. Reilly they speak of so highly,
Well upon my soul, Reilly, you're doing quite well.

Joe stopped working after a lifetime in a steady job. He had to adjust to living with the reality of a room full of knitting when his monthly pension turned out to be half of his working wage. He doesn't smile much and even less when his grandchildren help him check in on social media on his antiquated mobile phone.

His school buddy Bob and his wife Sue on vacation on the French Riviera turn him green with envy!

Not to mention the jealousy he feels towards Morgan, an ex-neighbour who lives in a lavish retirement home on a golf estate regularly posting pics of himself on the golf course.

He thinks, *AGGGHHHHHH!!!! Where did I go wrong?*

Social Media

Let's bring it into your world on a Saturday afternoon.

You're watching a news broadcast on TV. There's an ad break. A grey-haired couple is walking their handbag dog down a manicured path in a pristine retirement estate, smiling from ear to ear, glowingly healthy, with calming background music and the words '*This could be you at 65*' in a colourful, happy-looking font. The contact numbers, email address, and website link replace the contrived scene as the music fades, and the ad is replaced by the next one advertising a saving scheme to support your retirement dreams by the age of 65. If you continue watching the newscast, you will most likely have the same brainwashing ads thrown in your face several times.

When you've had enough of the news, you pick up your mobile phone to scroll through your Instagram feed. A friend has posted a pic of the great meal he enjoyed at a restaurant in Paris on vacation with his family. A twinge of envy pulls at your gut as you switch to search for info on travel to Spain. The following day, while you're scrolling Instagram, a sponsored ad from a bank pops up offering travel loans at zero interest. *What a coincidence!* You know you can't afford a holiday but consider the possibility of taking a loan from the bank that offers zero-interest loans for the holiday you deserve to take.

All of this in the space of a few minutes of the eighteen hours you are awake in a day, and there are still many hours left for you to watch news and movies, scroll social media, and get bombarded with more of the same.

There's not much ancient wisdom in social media research. Marketing companies provide statistics to assist companies in optimising their social media advertising, looking at the history of your scrolling from all angles. Hence the offer of a bank loan for your trip to Spain a day after looking at Spanish holiday travel. Social media will come under more and more scrutiny in the future. Until it does, it will continue to condition our minds into conformity. Everything in me, including ancient wisdom, tells me to be cautious of the influence of this force de frappe that would like to sink my FuM© ship.

It would be an unrealistic surprise to read this message in the final line of a social media ad offering you a low-interest loan covering a *fly now-pay later* travel deal including hotels and car hire:

ONLY IF YOU CAN AFFORD IT!

Rather than the standard bullsh$t:

BOOK NOW OR REGRET IT FOR THE REST OF YOUR LIFE!

How cool would it be to get a call from a bank manager or see an ad from a financial institution inviting you to:

Please pay us a visit, we'd love to discuss your:
Dreams for the future
Financial planning
Investment opportunities

And when you take up the offer, to be met by a warm-hearted person who looks you in the eye, offers you a seat, and begins with a personal *how do you do* enquiring about:

You
Your family
Your job
Your interests
Your fears of the future
Your dreams

Before getting into the financial talk.

Do banks even have managers anymore?

I quickly terminate telephone contact from a call-centre agent reading scripted questions like automated answering machines. I shudder to think what their response would be to a request for investment advice or anything not on the script. Other than hopefully helping you reset your security code, they will direct you to the *Frequently Asked Questions* page on the bank's website and terminate the call.

This is a loud call to arms!

REJECT CONFORMITY AT ALL COSTS!

Retirement Debunked

~~RETIREMENT~~

William Congreve wrote the play *The Way of the World* which premiered in March 1700 (ancient wisdom), in which it was concluded:

"The Way of the World *epitomizes the psychology of manner—the way people behave (hence the title). Motive is assumed to be the same for all: to get sex, to get money, and to remain young."*

And as more ancient wisdom tells us:

"There is nothing new under the sun."

And as *reality* shows us, the first two are attainable, but the last one is impossible.

Wikipedia tells us that the practice of retirement began in the 18th century when the Roman Empire provided a pension to their ex-servicemen. This is as far back as it goes. In the history of the world, retirement is a new idea, one that has failed us badly. My emphasis, rather, is on conserving the health of your min to enable you to think clearly and make good decisions. To rock your world enough to accept that you can navigate your future without the thought of retirement. It can become a *wonder-filled* reality for you by the time you read the last page of this

book. You will know when and how to say "F$CK YOU MONEY" without relying on the hollow promises of a shaky retirement plan.

That's right; you're going to reject an offer to make more money!

You're probably thinking, *This guy's nuts! He's lost his mind! Me, say no thank you to making more money? Never!*

I told you it would be a paradigm shift into a culture that transcends what you know and hear from advertising, cold calls, social media, family, and friends. I intensely dislike any advertising related to retirement plans that end with stories of disappointed and crushed lives because of the false promises. Bad advice given by people who have little or no real interest in your present or future well-being.

MORE ANCIENT WISDOM

Taking a cue from the Hebrew language which has also been around since 300 BC, I found that Hebrew speakers shared my dislike for retirement because they left the entire concept out of their thinking and vocabulary. I also believe that when there's no Hebrew word for something, it's because 'that something' is a bad idea.

No lies, there is *no* Hebrew word for retirement. The closest you will find is a word that is explained as *'working until one trembles.'*

So if you live long enough to tremble, then perhaps you *should* take a break.

Not everyone ends up in a state-run retirement home as Joe did. Some people end up comfortably enjoying a rest from the daily grind. But do you really want to sleep your days away aimlessly rocking in a chair on the porch of an old age home when there's adventure, excitement, purpose, and joy, just waiting to be had when you end your regular day job?

If you have a graphic mind like me, you would see a skeleton sitting in a rocking chair knitting bed socks. Not a pretty sight!

FuM© ***culture removes the idea of a comfortable, meaningless retirement.***

Step one is to remove the word from the FuM© ***vocabulary.***

RETIREMENT

The enjoyment begins when you start to plan and is indescribable when you end up living in the FuM© culture.

It will be very different from living life in unpredictable, short-term retirement.

ΔII PAUSE

This is not a pause for an ad break.

This is a real-life account proving all is not well in the state of Denmark, as Shakespeare's *Hamlet* warned us.

My mate Byron told me the sad story of his father who left school at nineteen and worked for an airline company as a maintenance technician. He retired a healthy man at the compulsory age of sixty-five. Unfortunately, Byron's mother was fighting a terminal illness. Their dreams of travelling to Europe in his retirement were shattered. First of all, her illness restricted any travel hopes, and second, the crushing medical bills ate into his retirement payout. Byron was in the financial position to help out with some of the medical bills and stepped in to assist. We have had some interesting discussions on the concept of FuM© since he shared his story with me.

It was during one of our chats that he shared the difficulty of one of his father's friends that shook me to my core and raised my hackles at the same time.

His name escapes me now, but he owned his own construction company. Fifteen years younger than Byron's father and not yet sixty, the age he planned his retirement to begin, his construction company ran into financial difficulties. The COVID-19 pandemic hit, and the severe lockdown restricted business operations for many long months. He lost some of his workforce to the disease as well, including his right-hand man, leaving him to rescue the ailing business alone. Forced to raid the company's savings, which soon ran out, he fell back on his personal savings. Paying off his remaining workers left little for him to live off. The savings soon ran out, forcing him into the only option of selling his assets to survive. His age kept him from accessing his retirement fund, and the contributions to it ground to a halt too. Hence, his eventual monthly pension at 60 would be drastically reduced. When the proceeds from the sale of the plant and machinery ran out, he ended up relying on his three children for support.

Thankfully these two men had children. What would have happened if they didn't?

I heard these two stories from *one* friend; can you imagine how many more there are around the world? I'm pretty sure that those two men saw countless ads in their lives about saving schemes at banks and guaranteed payouts from retirement schemes that lulled them into a false sense of security.

FuM© **would** have made the melodies of their lives so different.

What concerns me is how the world persists with the tired mindset of planning a retirement!

The definition of insanity:
Doing the same thing over and over and expecting a different outcome.

If you're climbing a ladder on a wall that leads to nowhere, move the ladder to another wall!

I was shocked recently to read about the increasing suicide rate in older adults. Dr Julie Rickard, a psychologist specialising in suicide prevention with teens and senior citizens, says that although the elderly constitute only 12 percent of the American population, they made up *18 percent* of successful suicides in 2021. Which is one in four of all attempts, compared to one in two hundred for teens. The reason for seniors attempting suicide is primarily to get rid of physical and emotional pain and the feeling of hopelessness. Some reasons that stand out are *Feeling like a burden to others* and *Food insecurity and financial troubles*. Doctors agree that depression is not normal for older citizens, as the myth goes.

My journey to retirement

Like everyone else, it began at birth. My claim to fame in the maternity home in Germany was topping the scales as the largest baby ever delivered there. My demand for milk had them preparing bottle upon bottle to keep me quiet after tossing the empty and crying for more. I still enjoy my food. The Germans loved me, stopping my mother in the street to get a good look at this unusual brown baby with the broad smile. I believe that this is where my love for people was sparked. My parents left India so my father could pursue a new career while furthering his studies in Europe. We lived in Germany for a short while before moving to Finland, where we stayed until I was four, when we relocated to the UK. My father's goal was to get to the USA, which took us to Chicago after a short spell in the UK. We lived there until he heard of a great prospect in Canada, the land of opportunity and promise that took us to Toronto. I was five and ready to begin my education.

It was like Nogg's nomadic life with his family, always looking for a new food supply.

Toronto was home until my father got another offer in Halifax four years later. Halifax is where I got my first taste of entrepreneurship, shovelling snow off driveways to earn some pocket money and supplement the housekeeping for reasons better left unwritten here. When it wasn't snowing, I expanded my entrepreneurial endeavours by dressing as a clown, painting my face, and performing at kids' parties.

Two years later at the age of eleven, we packed up and moved to Montreal in the state of Quebec, Canada. This move was traumatic for me because I left a school where I was doing very well, surrounded by a great circle of friends and satisfied with life. My mother, being the stereotypical submissive Indian wife, staying true to the culture, went along with whatever my father said. He put us in a situation where most of the people were French-speaking Canadians and basically disappeared from our lives. With no friends in a new community, plus an absent father, I was Nogg looking for an Aux. Mum and I formed a team and got on with life. I settled into my new school immediately, worked hard, and put myself at the top of the honour roll. I was a resilient kid, managing to cope with the change in environment and making new friends under difficult racially charged circumstances. It was in Montreal while I was at senior school that my working career began at the Holiday Inn. It helped that my mother worked there as a supervisor in the housekeeping crew. My jobs varied, eventually leading to senior roles in the food and beverage division. Working hard, I was driven to make as much money as I could and juggled school, sport, and work to maximise all three. I did very well to remain on the academic honour roll each year and played in the first basketball and soccer teams. The food and beverage manager always called on me for extra shifts because of my work ethic and my ability to do an excellent job for him. It supported my goal of earning as much as I could. I bought my first car, a Toyota Camry, for cash when I was seventeen, graduating high school.

Believe it or not, I was already planning my retirement.

My academic achievements got me into John Abbott College and McGill University, the beginning of my *real* education. I was set to study medicine but soon found out that I preferred financial studies and made the switch, against my family's wishes to have a doctor in the family.

I took to finance like a rock star to a stage!

I got my first permanent job in my final year at McGill when I joined Abbott Laboratories and met my first mentor, Garrick Killbery. He was *my* 'Aux', the first man I met outside of my family that took a sincere interest in me as a person. Garrick was willing to share his time, knowledge, and wisdom with me. He put a lot of trust in me at a tender twenty-three, which boosted my self-confidence and stretched me at the same time. The best advice Garrick gave me was when I was deciding to further my studies when he said:

"Bobby, do an MBA. You should get away from the family and be on your own for this. It will be the best for you."

I attended a great university in Ontario about eleven hours from home by car. By this time, I had replaced the Camry with a brand spanking new Toyota Tercel, also for cash. It clocked up many miles in that time driving home and back for weekends and university breaks. The move to Ontario for an only child who had spent the first twenty-three years of his life under the same roof as his mother and later his grandparents from India was very brave.

My wings proved to be strong enough to carry me, and my life took off into a world I consumed with a passion. Deloitte Touche Canada offered me a job as an investment analyst in Mergers & Acquisitions (M&A) on Bay Street Toronto. I took it and landed up back in the city of my childhood. It was a great job title to start a serious CV and the correct business address. Canada's equivalent of Wall Street. I was in job heaven. Until a consultant from Morgan Stanley noticed me on a joint project between the two companies and put my name forward as a possible candidate for a job with one of the biggest players in the market on Wall Street at an even better address than Deloitte's.

A twenty-five-year-old on Wall Street working with the world's best equity research team could never have been scripted in the plan for my life, other than in my dreams. It was a rollercoaster ride of excitement,

surprises, learning, stress, rewards, and everything I had seen in the movie *Wolf of Wall Street* that initially triggered my interest. I was on my way to being a millionaire with the vision of a comfortable retirement in my sights.

When the time came for a change, I left Morgan Stanley to join US Bancorp in Minnesota when they formed Piper Jaffray, entering the bulge bracket banking world. I was on the top of my game in the high demand arena of equity research. My Morgan Stanley credentials did the rest of the talking for me to land a great job earning good money. My plan to make and invest a lot of money to support a comfortable retirement improved with every new job I landed as I climbed the ladder of success. My life, however, took some unexpected excursions that led to me spreading my wings to look for a job in the UK. I wish I could say that I walked straight into a job there. It took a lot longer than I would have liked to eventually find a great job with HSBC and later an even better job, albeit reluctantly, with JCF. FactSet, an American company with a global footprint, acquired JCF, and the job turned out to be my ticket to independent entrepreneurship, having flexed that muscle making a pot of money for them and myself.

London was the beginning of a very interesting adventure, transition, adaption, and evolution into full-blown entrepreneurship and the conception of constructing my thinking into the eventual culture of FuM©. Like Nogg's evolution, it took time for my ingrained retirement thinking to deconstruct to prepare me for the mind shift.

Think of Nogg taking Jegg and leaving the clan on an adventure into his eventual FuM©. It wasn't clear to him, but all of the seeds had been planted by Aux to set him up for success.

It took us both some time before we figured things out in our heads. For Nogg, it began when he almost lost his woman and his unborn son, who were starving to death. I will reveal more of my path between these covers, beginning with the key lesson I learned that initiated the shift in my thinking. It happened when I got really serious about what I wanted my future to look like.

Sometimes a paradigm cannot be shifted unless it is blown apart and reconstructed. Mine was.

I WANT TO BE RICH VS CONTENT

Remember my mate Byron's two stories of failed retirement plans? When those two men started out all those years before, with the promise of travel and sunning themselves on exotic beaches, their answer to the question *"What do you want for your future?"* would probably have been:

"I want to be rich."

Rich people?

A snapshot of the global population of 7.9 billion people in 2021 proved the following statistics to be true.

2,755 billionaires	0.00003487%
56.1 million millionaires	0.710%
3.6 billion living on less than $5.50 a day	45.56%
That leaves pretty much the rest at	53.73%

All trying to be 'rich'!

The world is driven, to its detriment, by an affliction few are willing to admit. Even the poorest of the poor are caught up in it and would never be satisfied even if they came into a pile of cash by some stroke of luck.

I have asked you to exclude *retirement* from your vocab.

Now I am adding *rich* to the exclusions as well.

What a difference it would make if everybody strived for contentment rather than simply being *rich*!

How many living on \$5.50 a day aren't actually content? Some of them might already be saying "F$CK YOU MONEY".

"Sounds nuts!" you say.

What if the person owns the mud hut they live in? It is situated next to a perennial spring of crystal clear water. They eat one meal a day (which costs around \$1.50). They teach illiterate elderly people to read and write. Support their orphaned neighbour with \$1 a day and have the most gratifyingly restful sleep every night?

The ultimate state of independent contentment!

Accidental FuM©ers

Basil and Josh, without knowing it, wrote an FuM© melody.

They moved their ladders.

Basil, a friend of mine, has an interesting story of adapting and transforming his life when he contracted an ailment requiring constant expensive medical care. Not wanting to deplete his life's savings before he passed from this world to the next, he researched countries with affordable medical care as well as the basic daily cost of living. He was forced to look at what would be an acceptable level of independence that his finances would allow him to live on once the treatments were over. Looking at what would remain of his savings, he calculated what he could afford to live on and decided on a country to do it. Vietnam provided exactly what he needed, so he relocated and is sustaining his chosen independent lifestyle on the \$5,000 a month he can afford.

He placed his ladder on another wall—Vietnam.

Josh was defrauded out of \$27 million by some crooked lawyer he foolishly trusted to take care of his future. He ended up with very little of his amassed fortune and moved in with some kind friends in Swaziland, a tiny, landlocked country in the South of Africa, just to get by until he could sustain himself again. He fell back on his passion for writing and soon made enough money to afford a place of his own. After that harrowing ordeal, he set himself up so that he does not have to rely on the money he earns from writing. He is living an independently comfortable life on a meagre $400 a month as happy as Larry. He saves the rest, intending to use it in the future to set up a school for aspiring young writers from disadvantaged circumstances. Josh harbours no grudges towards the person who stole his money. On the contrary, he is grateful for the change in mindset that it has brought about for him. Where his previous life before FuM© was driven by greed, he now lives in peace with his circumstances and turned his selfish goals into generous philanthropy. His needs are met by an income that covers a $400 monthly budget to sustain his chosen independent FuM© lifestyle.

Josh can say yes or no to anyone or anything that offers him more money to add to his philanthropic endeavours.

He also placed his ladder on another wall—FuM©.

←← **REWIND** 200,000 years

I am reminded of a part of Dudd's life story when he was living in FuM© status as Nogg had modelled to him. He was lazing in a cool pool on the river to escape the blazing afternoon sun in Duddville when he heard a rustling noise coming from the bushes. All of his senses tingled as he edged towards his spear lying on the bank. From the noise in the bushes, he estimated the beast to be the size of a cavebear. When the bush suddenly opened up, a man emerged holding his spear drawn back across his chest, gesturing peaceful intent. Laying the spear on the ground, he stepped over it towards Dudd. A long series of grunts and sign language followed by way of asking Dudd to come to his cave and show him how to cultivate a crop of berry bushes in return for meat and skins.

Dudd's response was swift and harsh. Shaking his head vigorously, he waved an outstretched hand, rejecting the offer. He was effectively saying, "F$CK YOU MONEY!"

More meat and skins were not going to tempt him out of his contented independence. He ended the discussion and slipped back into the pool to continue enjoying his afternoon dip.

What a privilege! No peer pressure, social media, banks, insurance companies, parents, or neighbours brainwashing him into believing he had to do anything besides take care of himself, his family, and his ongoing well-being.

Continuing his quest, the caveman headed towards Nogg's cave, where the reception was friendlier than expected. Nogg was past striving for FuM©; he was into leaving a legacy for his family and giving back to the community, like Aux, his mentor. He agreed to help, packed a few things, and went off to teach the man some of his skills. When his job was done and the man wanted to pay him, Nogg turned him down politely and also said "F$CK YOU MONEY" to the meat and skins with a broad smile.

Nogg was the first philanthropist in this evolving world.

∆ **PLAY**

When Basil and Josh began their plans for future contentment, it began with a new awareness.

An awareness of something that few people ever get to embrace: the need to plan a future life of independence. A future where they will be free to decide how they would spend their days after arriving in FuM©. A timeframe set when planning their journey.

Any thought of retirement had been removed from those plans.

Like me, they never labelled the lifestyle they were planning when they set out to create it. They did, however, remove retirement from their vocabulary to create what I have called FuM©. Their success was made possible because they thought of their future needs without any outside influence from social media, peer pressure, or ideas of preconceived grandiosity. It was simply about what would make them independent and satisfied with life. There is no resemblance between the lifestyles of these two gentlemen and any social media rock star. We will never see either of them splashed on social media or interviewed on Celeb TV. They have nothing to prove to anybody and wouldn't get any 'red hearts' or rising flames on an Instagram post either. They don't need it because their well-being comes from a place inside them, not from any external validation or fame-seeking aspirations. Somehow, they were like Nogg a few million years before.

Evolution in reverse.

It's a great pity that Nogg never wrote a book and left it under a rock for us to discover his secret to avoid ever falling into the trap of retirement. Having no cold storage was his saving grace. He had nowhere to store food for more than a day or two. If he did, he would have had the same dilemma regarding the question of how much to store up for an uncertain lifespan that we do. As a result, he nurtured whatever he had and kept reproducing it.

I hope you're getting the message that the culture and paradigm of FuM© is an evolutionary process, not a panacea to obliterate the thought of retirement.

Well done, Nogg, Dudd, Basil, and Josh!!!!

Well said, Oscar! I could not have put it better.

> **True contentment is not having everything, but in being satisfied with everything you have.**
>
> *Oscar Wilde - Irish wit, poet, and dramatist*

How many mornings do you wake up feeling content?

How many mornings would you like to wake up to be as content as Oscar Wilde defines it?

You can, when you reach *your* FuM©.

What looked to you like an offensive, attention-grabbing book title teasing you to curiously pick it up and take a peek is actually the golden key that will open a door to your independent, contented future.

Don't you want to be independently content and have the freedom to say, "F$CK YOU MONEY!"

I'm not saying that millions of people on the planet working regular jobs, making lots of money, and saving for their retirement don't or won't enjoy the fruits of their hard work. If I let the statistics do the talking, they tell us the percentage that succeed in doing it as planned is as low as six percent. I say there's much more to life, and the culture of FuM© is the alternative option I choose to live mine in, with all of those who want to join me.

←← **REWIND** 200,000 years

Dudd had the option of accepting an offer in return for some skins and some meat. He said, *"No thank you."* Perhaps not so politely. But then, he was an abrasive caveman.

Nogg was at the next level of FuM© of making a difference in his neighbour's life.

The standard answer from my kids when I ask them if they want more of something is, "No thanks, I'm good."

They live in FuM© for now being taken care of as all young kids should. As they grow up, they will plan their future. I cannot tell them what it will be. They will decide for themselves. My advice to them will be the same as to you.

Once you scrap the idea of retirement, you can think of a future lifestyle of independent contentment. You have the freedom to accept an offer of earning some cash or simply say “F$CK YOU MONEY” and “No thank you” to the offer.

Why be happy when you can be content?

Abraham Maslow, an American psychologist from the ‘70s, is famous for his self-actualisation theory of ranking a person’s needs by firstly dividing them into three groupings: basic, psychological, and self-fulfilment. Under the basic needs, he placed the physiological needs of food, water, warmth, and rest. Safety and security make up the minimum for survival. Under the psychological aspect, he placed a sense of belonging and being loved before the need for esteem boosters like prestige and accolades. Finally, at the top of the pyramid under self-fulfilment comes reaching the achievement of our full potential and creativity.

Maslow’s findings are accurate in all respects when we stop to ponder the hierarchy and indisputably proven true in a long-term university study referred to earlier.

The Grant Study

Harvard University is conducting one of the longest ongoing adult development studies that began in 1938 during the Great Depression. ‘The Grant Study tracks a selection of 268 Harvard alumni from varying backgrounds to understand the secret to living healthy, contented lives. In a recent update on the study entitled *‘Good genes are nice, but joy is better’*, findings were taken from the remaining nineteen of the original group, all in their mid-nineties. The original group included men like President John F Kennedy and *Washington Post* editor Ben Bradlee (unfortunately, women were not included because Harvard was all

male at the time). The study was later expanded to include the men's offspring, resulting in a group of 1300 who are now between 50 and 60-something.

The study primarily includes parameters to find out how the experiences in the early stages of their lives affected health and ageing over time. There are some great stories of men going on to become successful businessmen, lawyers, doctors, and bankers. Unfortunately, there are also sad stories of some that ended up schizophrenic, and others addicted to substances, etcetera. Findings have surprised the researchers, of which some have only joined in recent years, while others have passed on—not surprising for a study spanning 83 years.

The end result of monitoring health trails and broader life incidents that included triumphs and failures in careers and marriages revealed that *relationships* and *happiness* in those relationships powerfully influenced their general state of health. The comment below comes from the psychiatric aspects of the study carried out by members of the Harvard Medical School.

"Taking care of your body is important, but tending to your relationships is a form of self-care too. That, I think, is the revelation."

It was found that those who were most satisfied with their relationships at the age of 50 were the healthiest when they reached the age of 80. The facts revealed that close relationships keep people happy throughout their lives, more than money or fame. The solid connections are a protection against the dissatisfactions that life throws at us. They help to delay physical as well as mental degeneration.

You would be right to ask why this is so significant.

Simply because these findings are a concrete guide to living a full, happy life compared to the normal measures of a person's social class, IQ, or even genes. It has proven true across the board for the original group of Harvard alumni as well as those added to the group over the years. Life is not as much about esteem and external achievements as it is about the human factor. The important ingredients to build into a legacy will be covered in detail in the latter part of the book as we learn more about the FuM© culture that is a practical way of life for *anyone* to achieve.

The study also showed the opposite to be true:

Those who lacked relationships and warm connections were not as healthy, died earlier, suffered more mental deterioration, had poor memory retention, and drank and smoked more. A disturbing but not surprising comment comes from a TED talk by Robert Waldinger, the director of the study, who said:

"Loneliness kills; it's as powerful as smoking or alcoholism."

Isn't it interesting that 50 is the age intersection for satisfaction affecting long-term health?

Reading another article related to The Grant Study, I found that some researchers have taken a deeper look at the semantics of the word *happiness* used in the study. They came up with a revision that resonates with me, replacing happiness with the concept of well-being. This resonated loudly with me as I reflected on times in my life when I was happy and thought it would last forever and came to realise that the feeling was fleeting and elusive. Psychologists have studied the difference between happiness and well-being because they must have felt the way I do. One of the psychologists wrote an amusing account of an experience that led him to ask about the difference between the two and emphasises the fact that we should be pursuing well-being as opposed to happiness.

(Edited by me)
Several decades ago, when he was in the period of emerging adulthood, the psychologist experimented with a psychedelic drug that ranked right up on the highest platform of happiest nights of his life. It happened

to be an historic occasion in the world of heavyweight boxing as well, which made it more memorable. Buster Douglas defeated Mike Tyson on that night, and it seemed like the event was a great victory in terms of good over evil in the history of mankind. The world was a better place to be. The group of friends he was with shared the euphoria of the moment for more than a moment.

He goes on to say that for a small cost, the drug gave him the happiest night of his life to that point. Yet he never repeated the use again and asks himself now, why not?

In using a psychological study that combines economics to explain happiness, the assumption is made that the root calculator of our investments is pleasure and pain. This means that the basis of what we try to accomplish with our actions is to maximise our pleasure and minimise our pain. It turns out in these studies that there are two systems of mental activity that relate to feeling good. Firstly, actually experiencing the here-and-now of the feeling, being in the present moment. Secondly, remembering, reflecting, and narrating it, which will decide how satisfied you are with the experience. This way uses the reflection to decide what was good for you. They are very different from each other. One psychologist in particular concludes that the first system is more accurate in assessing the experience based on the sum of the experiences in the here-and-now as opposed to the reflective rationalizing system because it can trick you into believing that something is better than it actually was.

He then paused and asked himself another question.

If for a small sum of money, I had one of the happiest nights of my life, why did I not do it again? He says that concern for the law, possible negative side effects from the drug, or difficulty in obtaining it played an insignificant role in his decision. Rather, he thought of it as having the option to be plugged into a pleasure machine providing constant bliss for the rest of his life. Would he opt for that?

Research again shows that neither he nor most other people would.

The focus on well-being, of which happiness is a component, consists of the crucial element of self-conscious reflection. Then there is health, personal functioning, and the environment that complete the picture—not forgetting what an individual values and ultimately believes that makes their life good (well-being).

> ***"The highest good is happiness with the worthiness to be happy."***
>
> *Immanuel Kant - German philosopher*

The salient point being that happiness is important but not all there is to well-being, and neither is it the only thing you should place value on.

Happiness must be justified.

Well-being is a great synonym for contentment, which leads me to a very interesting look into the framework around FuM©.

THE QUESTION OF AGE

Having scrapped the idea of retirement, I changed another paradigm when I looked at what society accepts as an appropriate retirement age.

Who says that 62 or 65 is the correct age to exit the productive work environment and live on your pension pay out?

Why put a whole age group of humans into neutral with their engines idling so they can coast placidly downhill into their graves?

Picture this: millions of people accelerating downhill in coffins on wheels without any brakes to stop them and get out to go back to the top of the hill and live an exciting life.

Try and wipe the picture out of your mind!

FuM© has no age delimiter because it is not focused on money. It is a non-prescriptive independent life of well-being with the means that you decide will provide contentment.

I say the sooner the better. Why wait for 65?

Having said that, I am not by any means encouraging you to jump ship out of the job market before you are ready because you *feel* like experiencing a state of well-being and contentment without the means to sustain yourself. It could be longer than you think before you depart this dimension for the next. I am simply suggesting that you remove the boundary of age from your planning.

You *can* choose the time in your life and plan for the age *you* want to live a purposeful life, doing more than playing golf every day or knitting bed socks, decaying from the inside out.

We are living in times when the number of millionaires is growing daily, and the age of these wealthy individuals is dropping. In the US, there were close to 22 million of them in 2021 with the greatest year-on-year growth of any nation.

According to the Global Wealth Report from the Credit Suisse Research Institute published by Investopedia on January 23, 2022, there was an increase of 1.7 million new US millionaires in 2020. This figure made up almost one-third of the 2020 global increase from 50.8 to 56.1 million. This was a massive rise of 5.3 million. The prediction is for the number of millionaires to reach 84 million by 2025.

Investopedia has ascribed the increase, which took place in the last half of 2020, to the rise in the stock market and soaring real estate prices. Also reporting that Americans under the millionaire bracket showed a six percent gain in wealth to bring the average worth of the American adult to $79,952 coming out of the same report. Another aspect to take note of in modern-day economic evolution.

Imagine how many Noggs and Dudds there were by the time the comet hit?

Here's an interesting piece of information that came from a report compiled by Ramsey Solutions, in which they found that only three percent of new millionaires inherited their money. That leaves a massive 97 percent who created their own wealth. They also reported that close to two-thirds of American millionaires never attended Ivy League schools. Rather, they came from public or state schools.

Zippia Research found a little over 8.8 percent of the US population to be worth more than $1 million. And on the topic of wealth related to age, they tell us that the average age for women who have $1 million set aside for retirement is 58.5, while for men it is 59.3 years of age.

There are differing opinions on the subject of retirement and death, but there is a common thread. Bearing in mind that studies refer to an unpredictable retirement that is generally spent selfishly consuming all of the money or leaving it to the family. If you retire at 65, you have a diminishing chance of living between ten to thirty more years. Averaged out, this gives you twenty years to provide a sustainable, comfortable, quality life for yourself with some opportunity to give something back to humanity.

This is no more succinctly illustrated than by Victor Frankl in his 105-page book *Man's Search for Meaning,* which is based on years of psychiatric research. Most importantly, the majority of his research came from observing fellow inmates in Nazi concentration camps during the Second World War, not from day-to-day society. He talks about two different mindsets of the prisoners, which I apply to FuM© culture. Some set a goal of being released by a specific point in time, like Easter, Christmas, or the next winter. When the particular milestone passed without their release, their disappointment led to such severe depression they lost their will to live. Fulfilling their ultimate wish, they died. In stark contrast, those who decided to take life on a day-to-day

basis and made a point of assisting others and projecting the positive hope of eventually reuniting with family and friends when the war ended flourished, despite the awful conditions. Many of them survived until the end of the war, if illness and malnutrition didn't take them before then.

This is powerful lesson is an integral piece of the beautiful mosaic that completes the DNA basis to form the perfect FuM© culture: a culture of well-being that thrives on a life filled with purpose and meaning.

How many of the 56.1 million millionaires in the world will make it past their greed, selfishness, comfort zone or simple complacency to make some small difference in the world?

With a changed mindset, they could live in the FuM© culture and start giving back to make a difference in the world.

Ever more people today have the means to live, but no meaning to live for.

Viktor Frankl

You will find this report from *elderGURU*, an organisation founded in 2009 by Derrick Grant interesting if you share my sentiments about making a difference as long as I can. The ageing-related research is provided to social workers, long-term care administrators, and case workers. The purpose is for them to understand the needs of older adults benefitting from Medicare to live the best life possible.

I believe we should be working on strengthening and empowering future generations, not trying to prolong our lives.

They made some interesting discoveries that reinforce the need for abolishing retirement to establish the new culture of FuM© freedom.

Combined with the average ages of men and women with $1 million set aside for retirement, these edited extracts from content written by Derrick Grant on the *elderGURU* website reinforce the need to debate age-related FuM©—the time when you start living your meaningful life, or in their case, retirement. Bear Victor Frankl's findings in mind while you read this article.

Social Security has noticed the trend that men retiring at 62 have a 20% higher likelihood of death than the general population.

One study looked at groups who retired at 65 and found that lower-status workers were more likely to die within three years of retirement. Higher-status workers lasted longer, averaging four to five years after retirement.

And here's the biggest kicker for FuM© living*!*

If their identity came through work, they found it harder to adapt after retirement. They were lost, insecure, and unsure of who they were and what they should be spending their time on. The result was an increase in alcohol consumption and depression.

Healthy workers that continued to work until they were 66 had an 11 percent reduced mortality risk, and even if they had health conditions, they still had a 9 percent reduced mortality risk.

They put it down largely to the abrupt change in lifestyle. And this strengthens the argument for *easing* into FuM© **way before you get there. If you incubate the meaning of** FuM© **before you reach the** time, it will be a celebration of the anticipated status you have been working toward. Your mind will be wrapped around the lifestyle already with established relationships to continue doing life. Socialising, enjoying a drink, smoking a hand-rolled Cuban cigar with good friends, attending sports matches, live theatre, and enjoying great meals in fine restaurants *should* be on your agenda. There's nothing wrong with

having a bucket list for your FuM© **to fully enjoy the culture because you have the means to do it.**

Regular connection with good buddies is essential. Too many retirees live a cul-de-sac life that ends prematurely in a state of meaningless boredom. It's a great time to play chess and bridge to keep the grey matter stimulated. Something I enjoy, especially when it includes my broader family, is travelling a few times a year when the kids are on school vacations. I've never tried my hand at it, but art is a great way to spend the free time you will have available. And of course, getting involved in meaningful activities like volunteer work or creating something of your own to make a difference in the community, the country, the world.

"If I am going to make a difference in my FuM© years, I want to be around long *enough to make an impact, setting up an infrastructure for it to continue when I do pop off."*

If you're still unsure of the concept of FuM©, don't worry. My transformation and paradigm-shifting I am sharing with you took time to evolve.

FuM© is:

An exciting journey that begins with a decision to discard the option of retirement

Uncomplicated - VERY PRACTICAL

A destination of contented INDEPENDENCE you set on your radar

The fruits left in a legacy of making a difference—finding meaning

A path to fulfilment waiting to be found by everyone

All about sustainability

Taking calculated investment risks, gaining knowledge, research, leverage, markets...

A new way of doing life

FuM© is NOT:

A monthly budget

A monetary amount

A greedy chase after money

A monthly income earned from working

A game of speculative risk

A silver bullet to financial freedom

A date on a calendar 65 years after your birth

A retirement fund

A meaningless pursuit of happiness

A windfall lottery winning or the proceeds from gambling in a casino—the win might be large, but the source is unsustainable

A daily investment management job

Each individual living in FuM© will have a unique experience. It's not a set recipe for how you live your life as much as it is a lifestyle. Take a good look at the 'NOT' list again to make sure of the criteria that are not part of the foundation. Sure, you have a monthly budget but not as you used to while you were gainfully employed. Your FuM© budget is a closed circle of the costs that have been calculated to cover your needs for the month, which are funded from passive income streams (a subject still to be covered). It is not a willy-nilly withdrawal of money to spend on every whim and fancy that comes along, especially those influenced by the scourge of social media.

Think excessive luxury—vehicles, yachts, massive homes ... Do you really need them to be content?

Your daily activities will not be dictated by an employer, uncontrollable debt (a subject for future discussion), a shortage of cash, social media influence, or anything other than what living in contented independence lets you decide.

It is well thought out, carefully planned, long-term focused, disciplined, well-managed and patiently executed.

Now is a good time to picture yourself doing whatever you would like to float your boat in FuM©. I know that looking further than a day or even a week ahead is something few people do. Relax, there's no rush. It is thinking about what you want to be doing in ten, fifteen, twenty, twenty-five... years from now when you're saying,

"F$CK YOU MONEY!"

Go on, it's time to dream a little.

I would like to

....

....

....

....

....

I would also like to

....

....

....

....

And I would like to

....

....

....

....

....

I am surprised by some people's dreams when I ask this question. Here are a few.

Art—painting, sculpting, ceramics...
Radio announcer
Sommelier
Brew master
Voiceover artist
Mental health counsellor
Rancher
Animal breeder
Open a coffee shop
Build an orphanage
Chef
Winemaker
Cannabis farmer

I find that it helps to frame the question with the word

'*actually*'.

It's not what you *think* you want to do.
It's not what you *see* in front of you to do.
It's not what *someone else* wants you to do.
It's not what you *think* someone else wants you to do.
It's definitely not what *social media* tells you to do.

It is what you *actually, really, honestly* would like to do!

In Jacob Nordby's non-fiction book *Blessed Are the Weird,* he asked himself and his audience a similar question. A question we should all regularly ask ourselves.

What do you *really* want?

> ***"These pure impulses get filtered through our conditioning and show up, distorted at times, but follow them back to their source and nothing you desire is anything but good and possible."***
>
> *(Jacob Nordby)*

He clarifies it with:

Did you know that every single one of your desires is an expression of your soul's longing to experience human life as you?

Yes, as YOU!

The question to ask now is, *How do I get there?*

The answer is: *Passive Income.*

Before we go there, I must clarify two very important points on the 'FuM© IS' and 'FuM© IS NOT' lists.

Calculated risk is the BEST way to a sustained FuM© investing *regime—as opposed to the alternative profiles of speculative risk, which is tantamount to gambling and exposing yourself to chance. This type of outcome may have the potential of a high level of upside growth but most definitely a very high level of risk.*

Speculative risk is a flawed mindset that corrupts a person's thinking into a state of invincibility. Bitcoin has been one such vehicle in the last decade that has bankrupted many investors, making them think that it is easy money.

Take this example from the LISTVERSE website published under the heading of '10 People Who Couldn't Handle Becoming Rich' on June 18, 2022.

Jack Whittaker *was a wealthy, successful business owner in the construction industry. In 2002, he won the Powerball multi-state lottery jackpot worth around $315 million. Jack, however, opted for the option of a once-off cash payment, leaving him with over $113 million after tax. Being a kind-hearted, well-meaning man, he pledged 10% to Christian charities and set up the Jack Whittaker Foundation from where he distributed food and clothing to the needy in rural West Virginia. He generously rewarded the man who sold the winning ticket and drove around the neighbourhood throwing cash from his newly purchased sports car.*

In 2003, someone stole over $500,000 from his car in a strip club parking lot and it continued to get worse for the man. His granddaughter's eighteen-year-old boyfriend's dead body was found in Whittaker's home after a drug overdose. Later the same year, his granddaughter suffered the same fate. Jack's gambling addiction didn't help either, and his uninsured house burned to the ground. He died in 2020.

Always chasing the illusive speculative risk of gambling is not only restricted to the lottery and casinos. There are piles of tempting investments, including bitcoin, to tempt you into a shortcut.

The fundamental basis for FuM© investing rests on *calculated risk.* This presents an outcome that has been well thought through by doing significant research on the various scenarios.

By analysing the risks, FuM© investing allows proper asset liability monitoring (ALM), which ultimately ensures that the return on your investments cover all the pre-determined liabilities.

My success has been achieved by steadily monitoring my FuM© investments and resisting the urge to intensely manage them every day—something that could sway me into making detrimental knee-jerk decisions. It isn't a daily check in the refrigerator to make sure you have enough milk for your cereal. It is a long road trip for me with my eye on the significant milestones and road signs to keep me going in the right direction. The potholes were avoided in time, and flat tyres quickly repaired.

"FuM© does not *expect you to be an investment wizard with three computer screens nursing your investments every minute."*

Definite Do's

- ≈ Get a mentor
- ≈ Have a long-term vision
- ≈ Be prepared to change paradigms
- ≈ Adopt a '*money works for me*' attitude
- ≈ Plan well
- ≈ Stay focused
- ≈ Make sound, calculated investments that generate income to match your obligations
- ≈ Be open to new ideas such as *alternatives*
- ≈ Forget about retirement
- ≈ Dream about a contented future
- ≈ Leave a legacy

Definite Do Nots

- ≈ Be lazy
- ≈ Be greedy
- ≈ Be in a hurry
- ≈ Be arrogant
- ≈ Be fooled by social media
- ≈ Be anxious
- ≈ Sweat the small stuff
- ≈ Lose focus
- ≈ Miss an opportunity to build passive income
- ≈ Follow get-rich-quick schemes

PART TWO
The Walk

Aesop, a Greek fabulist and storyteller credited with a number of fables now collectively known as *Aesop's Fables,* is another provider of the ancient wisdom that forms an important thread of FuM© culture. One such story that teaches us how not to jump to conclusions based on what our natural perceptions tell us is 'The Hare and the Tortoise'. At face value, the hare should win a foot race with a tortoise hands down. The metaphor for life, rather than the race is exactly how a walk into FuM© is unique to each individual. Whether you are a hare or a tortoise, you *will* reach the goal at your own pace. Looking deeper, the wise tortoise never tried to be a hare, and the hare could never be a tortoise. And the final lesson to be learned from Aesop is that FuM© is available to everyone who wants to participate. The slow tortoise was not excluded from the race, and neither was the hare set a handicap to match him with the tortoise.

I would like to extract some more wisdom from this ancient story that is fundamental to the positive outcome for the participants. Both the hare and the tortoise were willing participants in the race. Neither were forced or suddenly found themselves surprisingly thrust into the contest. I have seen too many failures of people who suddenly find themselves in a situation where they have much more money than they are accustomed to and have not acquired it through a dedicated, planned, committed endeavour. Take the lottery winners who blow their millions quicker than it took to purchase the winning ticket. Or a business venture suddenly taking off and piling up a quick fortune.

What about the gold-digger who marries a billionaire and helps them squander their fortune in a few short years?

You can rest assured that FuM© is available to anyone who is ready to write their music and add their own lyrics.

The hare will have a different *number* than the tortoise, and that's for them to decide. Two vacations a year to recharge the batteries would suit the hare's hectic pace of life, while the tortoise could get by with one. A lumbering old jalopy for weekly shopping for the leisurely tortoise would never satisfy the need for speed in a zippy sports car for the hare. A fancy split-level borough with room for a large family and visiting friends is the bare minimum for the hare, who frequents fancy restaurants enjoying extended lettuce and carrot lunches. A simple home-cooked bowl of grass will suit the tortoise, shared with a best friend in the shade of his favourite tree.

The career walk into FuM© is a unique one too. There is no set formula for success other than walking your walk, not anyone else's. Sure, there can be similarities. But no two will be identical. A trend I have seen with many careers is that the threads being woven from the start often combine into the eventual portrait of success.

A friend of mine recently told me about his cousin, whose medical career began as a nursing student. She continued studying until she had the credentials to open a specialised wound care clinic. She rose to international prominence in her field through the reputation she built up at the clinic. Now she travels the globe on behalf of some of the world's largest pharmaceutical companies, educating medical practitioners and promoting their products. She is also a regular speaker at international medical congresses.

I have met many successful people working in industries where they have exploited their early career experience to succeed at the top of their game.

I read an article about a young lady who pivoted from one industry where she thought her career would take her to making a living teaching job seekers how to go about the task of finding a job. This happened after she spent so much time job searching for herself that she became an expert at it. She eventually did find a job after learning from many mistakes and making corrections to her approach. After several months and hundreds of unsuccessful applications, she turned the job down and took a calculated risk, believing in her capability to pursue a new career. It was a case of *Been there, done that, got the job. Now let me show you how.*

She took everything she learned about job hunting and distilled it into the successful processes she now teaches job seekers with much success and enjoyment.

She has a new career she never dreamt of.

What you can take from these stories is to exploit what you have already achieved in your career or alternately to not miss the possibility of changing jobs. You can also find renewed energy and passion in a different industry, perhaps, related to your expertise but something you have never considered.

As you read on, you will notice the thread in my career that has been part of my walk each day. I never intended to follow anyone else's walk, but I was open to ideas and advice to guide me along the way. I firmly believe that we are all made up of energy, and we all radiate positive and negative energy. I allowed myself the freedom to connect with all the positive energy the universe had to share with me. This is what made my walk exciting, adventurous, and prosperous.

It *will* do the same for you.

MY WALK – I WANTED TO BE RAMBO

"You may try but you can't get away from what you really are."

"And what do you think I really am?"

"A full-blooded combat soldier."

"Not anymore. I don't want it."

"That's too bad because you're stuck with it. Let me tell you a story, John. There was a sculptor. He found this stone, a special stone. He dragged it home, and he worked on it for months until he had finally fashioned it into a beautiful horse. When he was ready, he showed it to his friends. They said he had created a great masterpiece, but the sculptor said he hadn't created anything. The statue was always there inside the rock, he said; all he did was chip away the pieces that weren't a horse. We didn't make you this fighting machine, we just chipped away the rough edges. You're always going to be tearing away at yourself until you come to terms with who you are. Until you come full circle."

Colonel Trautman managed to open John Rambo's eyes to see himself in the mirror, to see what he was: a combat soldier. The colonel pulled a great move just at the right time to get Rambo back in the game.

> ***Every block of stone has a statue inside it, and it is the task of the sculptor to discover it.***
>
> *Michelangelo – Italian sculptor*

Nogg did the same when he saw a farmer in Dudd and encouraged it out of him with the first seed he planted. It was what he needed to learn to become the provider of fresh produce he turned out to be for his family and his parents.

Rambo – First Blood

It's a quiet morning in Hope, the sleepy hollow in Liggett County. It will stay that way too if Sheriff Will Teasle has anything to do with it. He is the indisputable law in this town where everybody toes his line. Teasle's tolerance for unwanted outsiders is lower than a snake's belly. Cruising down the main road in his patrol car, he spots a long-haired backpacking drifter in a green US Army jacket walking into town. The needle on his tolerance meter jumps a few notches as he pulls up alongside the drifter and 'encourages' him to keep on walking. Rambo's dismissive response pushes the needle up another few notches. He orders Rambo into the patrol car and drives him to the town limits and drops him off with a curt farewell, telling him to get a haircut, repeating his advice to keep on walking.

An hour later, Rambo is being booked for vagrancy after ignoring Teasle's advice and returning to Hope to find some breakfast. Judging a book by its cover as Teasle did, all the cops in the station assume that they are dealing with a good-for-nothing, trouble-making bum. That is until they strip him naked to shower him down with a fire hose as per the boss's orders. They are stunned by the sight of Rambo's ripped six-pack belly and bulging biceps, but unfortunately for them and Hope, they still don't know what they are dealing with until they try to shave him with a cut-throat razor.

→→ FF

I'm on the edge of my seat. I want to slit Teasle's throat for treating Rambo like a criminal. He and his patrolmen are chasing him in the woods, trying to shoot him. Rambo has lured Teasle into an ambush. Turning the tables on him, he holds his huge knife at his throat and whispers his hot breath into the sheriff's right ear to call his thugs off. Showing that he is the better man, Rambo restrains himself from slitting his throat—not like I wanted to. He was brutal when needed and

restrained when he could have given in to his wild emotions. As much as he felt like taking Teasle's life, he still kept his cool and warned him to stop the war.

My chest swells with new respect.

The scene changes to the command centre which looks like a full scale war zone with military tents, radio equipment, armed vehicles and uniformed men crawling all over the place. All of this just for one man!

The outcome for both sides is a matter of survival.

"I've come to get my boy."

Sheriff Teasle shoots back, "Who the hell are you?"

"Sam Trautman, Colonel Samuel Trautman."

I was in the movie with John Rambo. No, I *was* John Rambo. I walked out of the theatre feeling exhausted, exhilarated, and relieved that I was still alive. As relieved as Rambo when he finally walked handcuffed down the steps of the sheriff's office with a trench coat draped over his shoulders. Colonel Trautman, the only man he trusted in the world, was by his side, taking him back home. I was there too, walking with him as the townsfolk stood and watched.

I was so impressed with everything about Rambo, the last remaining member of Colonel Trautman's Baker Team. His intense sense of loyalty, integrity, and passion for truth and justice drove him to destroy half of Hope to make the point that they had drawn first blood, not him. The scenes played over in my head as I walked home feeling the satisfaction of our victory.

I wanted to be Rambo!

Movies can arouse powerful emotions in us that stimulate our minds and bodies beyond imagination. I could not get enough of Rambo. His character lit up my being so brightly that I felt like people could see me in the dark. The sense of adventure was a small part of what I enjoyed about Rambo compared to the character of the man. His fierce drive for justice struck a chord deep within my soul. When I thought about how badly my father had treated my mother and me, I felt like Rambo when Sheriff Teasle's goons tried to beat him up for no good reason. It sounds drastic, but I felt as if I could easily take my father out with any of Rambo's weapons, including my bare hands. Rambo's loyalty, integrity, and courage came from his heart. He was a man after *my* own heart.

I was drawn into the movie screen as he sat on the floor in the police station in the final scene of *First Blood*. I was there with him as he spilt his guts to Colonel Trautman about how he felt being hunted like an animal in the mountains. How he had to fight for survival simply because Teasle disliked strangers in his town. My heart broke when he told the colonel how people had called him a baby killer at the airport when he came back from one of his tours in Vietnam. When on all of his missions serving his country, he gave everything he had to achieve success and lost all of his buddies in the process. I connected mostly with his drive to survive and his ingenuity to outsmart his enemies. There was nothing haphazard about the way he did things, sussing out a situation, planning his actions, and executing them. That has stuck with me to this day: assessing, planning, and executing.

Like any other kid in the theatre, the Rambo fantasy was reality that melted into my being. He was the real deal. The way he mastered his craft by continuously learning and adapting seemed like his weapons were an extension of his body, not just metal objects for combat. A ball became my weapon to use against the opposition on my battlefield: the basketball court. It felt as natural as an extra limb in my hands. I enjoyed the flow of the game as though I was in full control of my actions brimming with confidence. Without making the conscious decision, I started seeing my activity in sport and schoolwork as a mission to be accomplished. I focused intensely on improving my skills and becoming more aware of my surroundings, just like Rambo on the battlefield. I noticed things I had not seen before and often had scenes from the

movies flashing through my mind, especially in situations where I needed to make quick decisions. I disciplined myself to take care of my physical health too. Rambo instilled a deep sense of justice in me to fight for what is right. He hated injustice with enough vengeance to wipe it out.

I was always on the lookout for the release of the next Rambo movie and counted the days until I was sitting in the theatre watching my hero do what came so naturally to him. Colonel Trautman was my first introduction to the idea of a mentor, and a fine one he was. The lack of a father in my life, being brought up by a single mother, left me longing for male company. The colonel's words often replayed in my thoughts. A few, in particular, got me feeling as proud as Rambo when the colonel told him,

"You'll get a second medal of honour for this."

And

"You're the last of an elite group. Don't end it like this."

The colonel was very proud of what he had accomplished with Rambo.

What always impressed me was the trust between the colonel and Rambo, which is why Rambo could lower his guard and open up to tell him exactly how hurt he felt and what he really wanted out of life. He wasn't just a mechanical combat soldier; Rambo was dedicated to his country and the cause he was employed to defend. Whether it came from somewhere inside himself or if it was planted there by the colonel, John Rambo never understood or tolerated the word 'failure'. The battle wasn't over until he succeeded. My grandfather thankfully played Colonel Trautman in the movie of my life until I was old enough to make it on my own. Although I would give anything to still have him around today, I was blessed to have had him at all. Rambo's movie and mine would have played out very differently without his colonel and my grandfather in our lives.

My life mirrored Rambo's in so many ways. My mother did a great job without a husband to support us and a father to nurture me. I am really thankful for her and all of the sacrifices she made to give me a good education. But still, life was not easy growing up in a world where I had to make my own way and rely on myself to envisage a future where I would be free of the poverty that dogged my psyche for more years than I wish to remember. I had friends at school and university but often felt lonely. Like Rambo throughout his life to the end, living on his horse ranch, he was a loner and operated solo. My determination as you will read about got me into my dream job to the surprise of my family and friends. I pursued it relentlessly by making sure I got the education, including my MBA and CFA and any skills I needed to give me enough self-confidence. Enough to consider, at the tender age of 25, locked and loaded with great credentials and the balls to knock on a door. Not just any door—one that secured the entrance into the hallowed halls of Morgan Stanley, the global multinational investment management and financial services company on Wall Street in New York City, USA. The right address to move from to join HSBC in London, then move on to JCF, and end with FactSet before finally fulfilling my destiny. A fully-fledged entrepreneur running multiple businesses of my own, I know without a doubt that the central trait of self-confidence that Rambo and I share come from the same place inside us. We each had a mentor to guide us, but like me, he had a lonely childhood and also developed his character himself. Some were innate, and some I learned from Rambo.

Self-discipline

We likewise share more self-discipline than most. A consistent daily routine has always been part of my life since I was in junior school. It began with rising early enough to watch my favourite TV shows while eating breakfast before leaving in time to be the first one at school every day. I continue my regular routines to this day, rising early (not watching my favourite TV shows) and getting my day started before

anyone I work with. Sure, we have both had a few wobbles, but Rambo will agree that it's not about falling; it's about not staying down.

Rambo taught me a valuable lesson in the way he respected the colonel which is sadly lacking in life today. I followed his example in the way I respected my grandfather and accepted his input in my life. I respected my teachers and had good relationships with all of them, unlike many of my friends, who disrespected them. Neither of us would accept anything from someone we did not respect.

Rambo's influence plays out continuously in my life to this very day. My work ethic, my never say die approach, and my enormous passion and energy for living life to the full come from him. He has also had a lot to do with my transformation into the FuM© mindset. By example, he could never retire into an insipid lifestyle drawing a measly military pension, playing poker with a bunch of geriatrics and reminiscing on the war in a vet's retirement home. I learned from him not to think outside the box, but rather to throw the box away, following his example of taking calculated risks. Although we have never shared two words, Rambo is my vicarious mentor.

Before I begin telling you about the search, allow me to give you a look into the beginning of my personal transformation. The events that rocked and shocked my world. How I used my innate traits, acquired new skills, and got to know Bobby Rakhit better. How I found the path to get the most out of my career and set myself up for FuM©.

Michelangelo – Italian sculptor

LOOKING FOR A NEW JOB — NEW BUSINESS SALES

It's the 11th of September 2001, and the horrific 9/11 Twin Towers attack is playing out before my eyes in a boardroom at HSBC, where I work in London. The live broadcast unfolds as carnage, death, and destruction defy any reality of what looks like a well-constructed movie scene. The blood in my veins runs ice cold. I'm shivering like a leaf from head to toe, realising that I know people who work in those buildings. They could even be one of the jumpers flying out of the windows a hundred floors up, escaping the flames; choosing death by anything other than being burned alive. I am literally standing on the sidewalk in New York, sharing the shock with thousands of bystanders. I'm not even thinking of the ramifications on the global financial markets simply because I cannot comprehend what is happening in New York. I see flames billowing out of the North tower when I instinctively rock back in my chair as if Muhammad Ali has sucker punched me. It is 09:03 (GMT-4) when a second aircraft flies into the South Tower, exploding into flames.

What the $"#!*

I wish I could stop this history from unfolding on CNN. It is sending everyone in the room's minds into unfathomable havoc. If only we could turn it off and go back to life as we knew it before we turned on the screen.

I worked on Wall Street, less than a mile as the crow flies from the Towers. I've walked past them, and I've been inside.

Time blurs past in a haze, and I am on my way home with thousands of other commuters who are stunned, confused, and depressed.

It's the 12th of September, and life goes on. At work, I hear the same television broadcasts telling us that the global economy is crumbling as fast as the Twin Towers. Meeting after meeting spent speculating, adjusting, and collaborating across continents to understand the extent of the fallout. Scarcely having time to grasp my emotions that have taken repetitive Ali-like sucker punches and right hooks, it is the 17th of September, just six days later. I am standing beside a hospital bed in Canada. I am saying goodbye to my best friend, mentor, and grandfather Dadu before he breathes his last. I am grateful he held on long enough for me to get there before his passing the following day. Extremely grateful! HSBC kindly released me to fly home as soon as my mother called to tell me he was asking for me. In a surreal wave in time, my life flashing by sees me on a return flight home to London a few days later. Leaving my mother and grandmother to cope with their grief was as tough as saying goodbye to Dadu.

→→ FF six months

It is 2002, I am 29 years old and reflecting on getting my job out of university in 1997 when I was 24. It feels like a lifetime, but it has only been five short years. At the pace I live life, I have crammed ten years into five.

I'm still in London.

I have recently returned from a sabbatical generously sponsored by HSBC because of a vacuum in business caused by the downturn in the financial markets. It was just what I needed to help me recover from the trauma thrust on me in September. I used the time to soak up Europe's historical culture, street cuisine, and hospitality like a sponge. I discovered what life was really about after the sprint from 1997 to where I now found myself. Most of my previous travels were work-related, enjoying business class flights, five-star hotels, and Michelin Star dining. My sabbatical funding, in comparison, saw me flying on budget airlines, sleeping in backpacker lodges, and eating local street food. I got to know the citizens of the countries I visited, saw many small out-of-the-way villages, and enjoyed wholesome food in parks and sidewalk cafés.

Slowing down got me to a place where it was possible to get to know Bobby Rakhit. Without the accelerated thrust keeping me ahead of the poverty curve, I discovered what made me tick and what living life for me was all about.

It was an amazing journey of unplanned, unexpected, unbelievable discovery as I found—my authentic self. I have never had so much fun as I did getting to know so many wonderful people, exploring their world, and soaking up every new experience like a sponge. The Bobby who flew to Turkey on the first leg of my excursion was not the same Bobby that returned to London from my final European excursion. Europe was a significant phase of the rock-chipping transformation that resembled Rambo's walk when he saw himself as an average Joe. Before Colonel Trautman saw through the façade to destroy the average Joe persona and create a full-blooded Green Beret combat soldier, one chip at a time.

When HSBC gifted me a six-month sabbatical, I let the idea play over and over in my head like a sweet symphony. Little did I know at the time that as much as Rambo never understood that he was a combat soldier until the colonel told him, I was unaware that I was a competent globe trotter. It must have been the influence of "Come Fly with Me," one of Mum's favourite Frank Sinatra numbers. Little did I know I was embarking on a journey of discovering much more than what Europe had to offer. I was about to discover my true self.

The uncertainty in the financial industry after the crash led me to use the spare I had to look around for possible new jobs. It chuffed me to get a few offers while I was still employed by HSBC, which consequently restricted me from accepting anything until I resigned, possibly under restraint of trade, unless HSBC let me go. I was definitely not going to resign and give up my six-month holiday before it was over. Having worked hard at honing my equity research skills up to that point, I kept my job search focused on that sector of the market, notwithstanding

the massive turmoil it was in. Equity research is what I knew, and I was really good at it.

The sabbatical was the most significant six months of my life, flipping the switch to FuM© thinking. I kept hearing a voice in my head calling out to me saying....

"Will the real Bobby Rakhit please stand up!"

I was a young man living inside a bubble before my sabbatical, running as far away from the fear of poverty and the memory of living in a rundown rats-arse hotel as I could. Those memories were gradually stripped away, catalysing my transformation to reveal the real me. I never saw it then, but I subsequently realised that the events of 2001 were a vital part of the destruction I needed before I could become the person my next job needed me to be. The bits of rock were chipped off me like Rambo's combat soldier revelation. The final rendering of the statue living inside me continued in an interview for a job that presented me with a new career that eventually resulted in me writing this book.

I was born to be an entrepreneur.

A mutual friend who knew I was in the job market suggested that I talk to Colin Rogers at JCF, a company focused on financial information. Providence would have it that Colin would be the sculptor to take up the hammer and chisel and craft me into what he perceived me to be: his director of new business.

When I think back on all the interviews I had attended before, it was the first one where the *real* Bobby Rakhit showed up. I could not see myself as Colin did, but there was most definitely a *new business salesperson* in me waiting to be discovered. I was clueless about the job on offer or the domain Colin operated in until a very strange feeling swept over my being as we chatted. For the first time in my life, I didn't feel the usual fear of poverty that had been dominant in all my previous job

interviews. It was weird, unfamiliar, peaceful, relaxed, and a feeling I wanted to hold on to forever. I knew I still wanted to make a ton of money, but now it was for a different reason. I was hungry to succeed in the job, but it was not simply to assuage my fear of poverty with a big salary. I knew about being hungry to be successful from my early taste of entrepreneurship when I shovelled snow and sold my bike. I thrived on the gratitude of my satisfied customers with clean driveways and the look on my mother's face when I handed her the cash from the proceeds of the bike sale.

I drew another parallel for my life from Rambo's: his hunger for succeeding on a mission rather than being paralysed by the fear of failure.

The interview was more like a friendly chat than an intense interrogation. I felt comfortable enough to be vulnerable and share parts of my past and future ambitious aspirations and fears. Colin couldn't believe that I began my university studies in the medical faculty with my sights set on being a doctor before switching to financial studies and setting myself up for a dream career in investment banking on New York's famous Wall Street. He laughed when I told him about my first job in London while I was waiting for the job with HSBC. I worked for a telemarketing call centre trying to sell faceless people a financial product.

He smiled and nodded when I told him about my entrepreneurial endeavours as a kid in Canada. He looked doubtful about my brief attempts at landscaping and home improvements with a mate from the Holiday Inn. Selling my bike must have sealed it for him. He went quiet for a while before cocking his head to one side, nodding slowly and saying with a smile, "You know, Bobby, I see in you something I have not seen in anyone I've interviewed for this job. You have an entrepreneurial wick waiting to be lit. You would have been bored to tears in the medical profession, and I have a hunch that investment banking will not hold your attention forever. You are neglecting that desire in you. You need to unleash it on the world. You will do a great job in new business sales."

It was my turn to be silent for a minute, digesting his comment and enjoying the adrenaline rush set off by my childhood memories shared with him. I still wasn't sure what *new business sales* was about, so I asked him what he needed from me if I took the job. He told me he was looking for someone to crank up sales. I would be his new business sales director and should forget any reservations I had about having no sales experience. I abbreviated it to NBS to make it simpler for me, and he fleshed out some more detail.

He wasn't concerned about my skills because he saw traits in me that convinced him I was a good fit for the job and JCF, the company. Given the opportunity, I could do exceptionally well with it, far beyond my wildest expectations. My equity research background was an unusual asset for a person in the position he was offering me. My easy manner, social skills, and high level of EQ attracted him too. Besides opening up the market for him, Colin wanted me to infiltrate the London financial and media circles. I would form connections and gain exposure for the JCF brand, building credibility in the marketplace. He was sure I could establish a network and do whatever it took to convince a client to sign a deal. It sounded so simple. I still wasn't sure, though. He noticed my reticence and put me at ease, saying that I had nothing to lose and everything to gain from the challenge if I pulled it off.

The deal was clinched when he said, "You're a likeable guy, Bobby. If you take all the attributes I've mentioned and apply yourself, you will make a killing."

I don't know how, but Colin, the genius, saw who I was and what I wanted from life. Although FuM© was not part of it for me then. Just to assure me that he wasn't sugar-coating a bitter pill, he frowned, shook his index finger at me, and said, "I won't lie to you Bobby; new business sales is not for sissies. But in you, I see the heart of a lion. You will do well!"

←← REWIND 200,000 years

When Nogg stood above the waterfall, looking over the lush landscape at the water crashing into the river far below while Zugg lay starving with their baby in her belly, he saw the potential for a great future for them. He was at peace amidst the turmoil of the uncertainty waiting for him on his return to the bleak cave. Several million years apart, Nogg and I looked into our FuM© status without knowing it.

Colonel Trautman's speech was no different from Colin's comments about my future with JCF.

CIRCLING BACK

Changing lanes in my career sparked an interest in the stories of how people's careers take unexpected turns that lead to success. It interests me to see how some deviations are born out of necessity rather than following the planned path. I began by studying medicine and ended up as an entrepreneur breathing life into my FuM© vision. New business sales did it for me. Who knows what will do it for you? Perhaps you are in the ideal job to get you there, in which case, the decision will be to simply change your mindset about how you plan your future.

Unlike the walks we take with a planned destination, a career walk takes some twists and turns. Either planned or unplanned, they ultimately make up the walk. Mine began when I taught the investment team in the Canadian Imperial Bank of Commerce a course on Canadian Securities. They offered me a permanent job, which I turned down because I set my sights on bigger things. The first full-time job in my chosen career was with Deloitte Touche in Canada as an investment analyst in the Mergers & Acquisitions Division. This job set me up for my dream job on Wall Street with Morgan Stanley for the best equity research team in the world. Equity research became my forte, and I worked in several firms, always ambitious, looking to make more money.

From Morgan Stanley, I moved on to join Bancorp Piper Jaffray on their newly formed ER team. From that job, I changed countries and moved to the UK, where I landed the job with HSBC in London, still in ER. London introduced me to the international banking world and expanded the knowledge and experience I'd gained in the insular Canadian and US markets.

I put this experience to good use when I changed lanes into my new job in new business sales with JCF, that later became FactSet.

The Bobby Rakhit Brand emerged through printed as well as televised media. Colin Rogers set me off and then nurtured me through this phase to draw attention to JCF's products. He allowed me the freedom to test many of my untapped skills, particularly entrepreneurship.

Entrepreneurship

I will never forget when Colin told me he saw vibrant entrepreneurial energy in me. The drip-feeding I'd received as a child from selling my bicycle and subsequent input from the surrogate fathers in our friendship circle at the time was pertinent. They shared their daily business experience freely with me and cathected my spirit when I needed it. Circling back to my childhood, it occurred to me that instead of running around with my friends, I'd chosen to sit in the men's company with both ears open. The seeds that grew into Rambo's career grew from playing war games with his young buddies and watching movies like *The Bridge on the River Kwai, The Longest Day*, or my favourite, *The Great Escape*. His will to survive kept him going when his life balanced on a knife edge as he hung by his fingertips on the side of a cliff face, gritting his teeth while a crazy cop fired shots at him from a hovering helicopter. That drive came from somewhere in his life. We both actually began preparing for our eventual careers as young boys.

My connection with entrepreneurship at this level was not immediate because of the misperception that I needed to be the next Richard Branson to succeed. It was only natural considering my drive to make as

much money as possible to avoid poverty and retire one day. Branson owned a magazine at sixteen and went on to create record labels and airlines. I was working in the Holiday Inn at sixteen, and I never even had my own business.

Then I got to thinking and saw this scene in my mind from *Honey I Shrunk the Kids*. The dad shrunk his kids with the machine he invented. The kids stood eye to eye with a mouse. It changed my perspective to bring entrepreneurship into a relative focus of possibility in my life. I didn't have to be as big as Richard Branson. It's all relative, looking at the thousands of small business entrepreneurs in informal markets, the gadget shop owner in the local shopping mall, my Internet provider, who started as a computer technician straight out of school, and millions more. They all took risks creating their businesses and continue taking them daily to succeed and make a living, enjoying the fruits of their labour.

They are all Richard Branson creating something out of nothing.

It also occurred to me that the title of entrepreneur is not only for people with businesses. I have met hundreds of entrepreneurs that don't own their own companies. I was in a new pond where I would tread water for a while, gathering confidence and momentum before confidently swimming freestyle. I walked until I could run. It was my first real excursion into serious entrepreneurship before eventually establishing businesses of my own. I created a very successful business for Colin within a large corporate structure by building a team of people and managing them, plus taking the risk of losing my job if it didn't work out. I put my neck on the chopping block like any other entrepreneur.

←← **REWIND** 200,000 years

Nogg was the first ever entrepreneur when he created a family enterprise trading with the neighbours. His entrepreneurship boosted his FuM© status too. He set a perceived value for his produce to trade

for goods to the same value. He took the risk of opening up the borders of his territory to the possibility of hostile marauders that could have plundered his entire livelihood.

My life is still action-packed and fast-paced. I get things done. The excitement of equity research got my motors firing on all cylinders when I landed on Wall Street. My walk took me into NBS with Colin at JCF, by which time I had intimate knowledge of the finance industry. By providing relevant solutions through detailed research as quickly as possible, I moved into the fast pace of new business sales. All that was left for me to do was merge my research experience into my newfound selling skills to make a success of it.

I was fortunate that my career evolved from a firm foundation in the finance industry to a broader skill-set to match my enthusiasm for making a lot of money.

Rambo's drive and energy drove my hunger for success and encouraged me to take on the challenge on offer in my new career.

I was up for the challenge.

Bobby Rakhit, young buck, oozing testosterone, psyched up and ready for the first big deal to make my mark.

NBS turned out to be a perfect fit for the new Bobby, bringing some ready-made skills needed for the recipe to cook up the perfect dish for Colin *and* JCF.

Making my Mark – Settling in

Think Colonel Trautman preparing Rambo for combat, sending him into the battlefield and nurturing him until he finally left the service. We both did a great job for our boss. Rambo's first assignment in combat with live enemies, real bullets, and a big knife after his specialised training was the same as my first client meeting. We were anxious about the unknown and soon settled confidently into our respective roles. My

Rambo wish that was always with me morphed into his image, drawing on the traits aroused in the movie theatre as an impressionable kid. The only difference was that my business suit had replaced the makeshift combat gear.

Please allow me a quick diversion to share a funny story about my transition from a Canadian country bumpkin to a fashionably dressed Wall Street Equity Analyst at Morgan Stanley. It is about the outfit I wore on the first day of my New York job. The suit that was fashionably acceptable at Deloitte's back home looked like a potato sack compared to the tailored threads my colleagues were wearing. It hit me like a hammer looking at myself in the men's room mirror. I noticed the guy next to me looking at my reflection, a smile curling his lips as he straightened his tie and jacket, smoothing his neatly groomed hair to perfection.

Needless to say, my first paycheck was spent on suitable threads.

My NBS armoury, except for an expensive tailored suit, consisted of a laptop, my product knowledge, good social skills, and loads of enthusiasm.

I was as alert as Rambo, ready for action, challenged, excited, and hungry for success.

I was aware of everything going on in my surroundings, picking up cues, reading body language, and listening to the tone of my client's voice. I saw Rambo in the desert waiting for the enemy helicopters that were hunting him down, predicting the direction they would come from so he could find the best vantage point to shoot the arrows that blew them out of the sky. I was looking for the most opportune moment to fire my arrows and close the deal.

Tenacity and Perseverance

Two close relatives I possessed as naturally as Rambo's predisposition for adventure and achievement, often finding ourselves in sticky situations we never expected. How do you predict situations when you

run your life at a pace at which most mortals would lose traction and fly off the planet? Like Rambo, when I set my hand or mind to something, I focus all of my attention on the task. There is no pulling out until the job is done and dusted. No matter the mission, it was not a haphazard plunge into the unknown, hoping for the best. I saw this attribute lacking in my peers, which put me ahead of the pack. I never lost my mojo when I didn't close a deal; I went after the next one.

Adapting to the Environment

The first few weeks of my NBS career were like when I had seen Rambo in the unfamiliar forest above Hope with a bunch of barking sniffers closing in on him. He had never set foot in the place until then and used his skills, expertly adapting and orientating himself. I acquainted myself with the unfamiliar NBS environment, got to know the lay of the land, and stayed the course.

Remember how I had to unlearn my country bumpkin Canadian dress sense and adapt to the Wall Street fashion code? That set me up for when I expanded my FactSet empire to include India, to teach my uneducated staff about the unfamiliar corporate environment they had joined. The only difference was that I sponsored my recruits because they were not in a financial position to purchase the expensive tailored suits.

Relationships...

have always been easy for me to form, but the requirement of getting out of the office from behind a desk was the significant change needed to make it happen. It was a welcome change to get out and about and find a marketplace where I felt so at home. The second minor change was an easy one of using my very well-developed social skill of forming friendships and casual acquaintances to create connections with business clients. It is still a skill I exploit to transform business meetings from tense situations into less formal, relaxed experiences. I took to the role as gracefully as an eagle on its first flight and kept flying from there.

NETWORKING...

with the purpose of lead generation was no different to socialising with colleagues like I had done in school days and with friends like I still do in my everyday walk of life. For NBS, I contacted colleagues and friends to get going and then dug into the extensive list on my Rolodex that was full of equity research contacts from my time with HSBC. I always spend time finding out about my contacts' partners, significant others, and broader family, showing interest in life beyond the individual connection. I also made special notations of specific business requirements for the clients I met. It gave me an immediate edge over my competition because I could extract research data and construct financial models relevant to their business in the current climate. It was fresh, cutting edge, and unique to JCF's propriety software.

Every hero or successful person in NBS needs to have a wingman. I created a number of technically savvy nerds who I took to meetings to crunch numbers while I kept the client engaged.

SELLING MYSELF...

began early for me, complimenting my eleven-year-old entrepreneurial spirit when I ran my snow shovelling enterprise. Adults did not intimidate me when I knocked on their door to introduce myself and my services to them. I carried that same boldness into NBS as if I was back there knocking on doors for business. From the first call setting up a meeting to the actual event of signing the deal, forming solid relationships was easy for me. My new colleagues were confused. After years of making call after call trying to drum up new business sales, they were still in the starting blocks compared to me. Even Colin, who believed in me, was surprised at how quickly I turned things around for him and even more so when he saw me developing into an expert salesperson.

If you do a good job of selling yourself and forming relationships, you are doing a good job! The next big deal could come from a lost sale referral.

Word of mouth is the most effective marketing you will ever achieve!

The stars aligned, bringing Colin and me together at the precise time I needed to meet him. The JCF job seemed like a long shot, far removed from the job I was after. I took Colin's challenge on with guns blazing and my hunting knife tucked into my combat boot. Adapting a little more every day as Nogg did, getting used to eating meat daily from a diet of veggies and berries.

The ancient wisdom that iron sharpens iron described the fit between Colin and me. He continually sharpened my skills, taking nicks and scratches out, honing me to perfection. I responded by stretching myself into the role and his people management skills to trust me enough to do a great job with minimum supervision. I'm not shy to tell you, and he would agree that managing my energy and enthusiasm was a new experience that made me a handful for him to control. He never complained, though, because I made it worth his while by delivering sales as he had never seen before.

Creativity...

synchronised with my enthusiasm for the NBS job stirred the dormant skills I relied on to make a name for myself with my literary prowess in junior school. I could not have reached any level of sales greatness without it. Rambo's creativity kicked in whenever he needed it in tight situations, regularly saving his bacon. There was no time in the height of combat to park off in a comfort zone, lest he lose the battle or his life. I never took my foot off the pedal either, lest I lose a deal, or worse still, my job. We both used our creativity to the max to succeed. I am continuously looking for new challenges that take require every bit of my creativity to pull off.

Improvising...

was the name of the NBS game because it felt like I was suddenly in a pro football game, fumbling with an oval ball that often bounced

opposite from my expectations. I found it an exciting challenge compared to my colleagues, who complained about the volatility of client decisions. I never dodged the bullets; I simply asked probing questions to understand my client's needs so I could provide solutions. My deep knowledge of the product I was selling and the dynamics of using financial research made my job easy.

Education and passion

Were the final pieces of the Bobby Rakhit new business director job. They completed the requirement needed to increase JCF's sales and exposure in London's financial marketplace. My expert knowledge in quantitative research (QR) came from my intention to learn as much to support my energetic performance as I could. It was an aspect of my life that came naturally to me, beginning with my first exposure to formal tuition when I aced the entrance exam with excellent scores to get accepted into the Halifax Grammar School, a school my mother chose because she wanted only the best for me. I ended the year at the top of the honour roll and repeated the achievement every year to my final school year before college. I have never stopped educating myself and passing my knowledge on to others since the entrance exam.

Applying my passion for success in the job with my expert QR knowledge, I set to work getting myself into a situation that presented the perfect opportunity to fulfil Colin's mandate. One evening having a few drinks with a man who shared my passion for QR, he offered to introduce me to his colleague at the *Financial Times*. When the door opened a crack, I got my foot in quickly, and we got together. We shared interests, insights, and our research insights. It was a meeting of the minds that led to me writing articles for the *Financial Times*. The readers liked me, turning it into a regular Bobby Rakhit column. The writing gig got me invitations to appear on a Financial TV programme sharing my insights. Regular appearances led to more invitations from other TV channels, so the readers and viewers got to know Bobby Rakhit and JCF. I received

invitations to talk at business conferences to address some of London's top financial minds.

I built my brand–Bobby Rakhit, Quantitative Research Expert.

I was a product–I was in demand.

Mission accomplished:

JCF got exposure, and I expanded my already substantial network.

Doing Business

It's a fact that you become like the people you hang out with. I am drawn to like-minded people and love socialising with them as often as possible. It is no small wonder that my mates and I raise the eyebrows of people within earshot of our passionate conversations around financial research methodologies in restaurants and pubs, as the intensity of our discussion rises in proportion to our passion for the subject. I am always loudest and continually apologising to the surrounding patrons. It is a platform for sharing ideas on our business life in a relaxed setting, educating each other to go out and do a better job in the marketplace.

Rambo's influence is the inspiration for my *b@lls to the wall* approach to life, sustaining my passion for life, the universe, and everything wrapped up in and beyond my everyday existence.

I soon perfected my craft, closing deals with some heavyweight clients. My meticulous approach to the job garnered Colin's confidence in my ability enough to trust me and give me the freedom to run my own show and deliver the goods for him. I have always lived by my maxim:

There is no room for shoddiness in my life.

In one of our debriefing sessions, Colin commented on a trait I never knew I owned until then. Without it, I would not have been successful. The words rang in my mind for a long time after the discussion.

Cocking his head to one side and waving his index finger at me, he said,

"Bobby, my boy, you have a ruthless killer instinct. You don't take no for an answer. I love it, son; it's your biggest asset."

To which I responded,

"I am greedy, Colin. Greedy for money and success!"

To which he sternly replied, narrowing his gaze and nodding his head, still waving his index finger at me,

"Greed and hunger, Bobby, are what will put you at the top of the leader board!"

NBS made me come alive just like my sporting days when I was so in tune with my body and my ability to do well. It came back to me as if I was on the basketball court or the soccer field scoring goals again.

On the basketball court, I timed my passes to perfection and accuracy, swerving, dodging, and regularly adding points to the scoreboard. I was equally impressive on the soccer field and hockey pitch too. New business sales required accurate information and predictions for my clients' defined needs, timing the passes precisely (asking questions), waiting for a response, and scoring the goal (getting a signature on a contract). My Rambo-like killer instinct produced results, never satisfying the desire to win. I continually went for the next one.

In conclusion to my NBS walk, which was significant but definitely not the final stage of my walk, I want to leave you with a snapshot of the best part of the walk.

Meet Bobby Rakhit - New Business Sales Director (having fun)

I have always enjoyed a good party since I was a kid, having a lot of fun. I clowned for kid's parties to make some dough. Briefly tasting the excitement of entrepreneurship as a kid supplemented my allowance

and helped my mother with some housekeeping costs. But I made sure there was always some fun money in the kitty. My college and university days weren't short of the usual student shenanigans, and Wall Street took things to another level. Watch *The Wolf of Wall Street,* and you will see what I mean. My NBS career added intense flavour to my *fun history*. I wasn't joking when I said I knew nothing about the world of NBS when I began the job. It worked to my advantage, though, as I set about creating my unique signature in the realm of NBS. My winning streak took off like a rocket when I signed a deal with one of the largest financial institutions in the UK early in the walk.

The undisputed Heavyweight Champion of the World, Muhammad Ali, summed up a winning attitude when he said to an opponent one day,

"How tall are you? So I can know in advance how far to step back when you fall down!"

I never wanted to see the NBS cookie cutter, and Colin never showed it to me. I not only aimed to be super successful, but I planned to have loads of fun doing it. I was soon travelling all over the United Kingdom, recruiting new clients. I was away from home for twenty days a month, staying in the best hotels, dining in the finest restaurants, and signing record-setting business deals. I celebrated my success by drinking premium brand champagne and smoking hand-rolled Cuban cigars. I met film stars, sports legends, and rock stars. I was mistaken for and treated like a Bollywood film star more than once. I lived Dean Winters' saying: *"I work hard, so I play harder."* Playing hard was part of the Bobby Rakhit NBS culture.

Working hard wasn't restricted to the job, I must add. Late nights, long lunches, and being the first one in the office in the morning doesn't just happen because you say it must. I worked out in a gym before work every morning. Rising early has always been the norm for me. Late night or not, I was in the gym for a workout and a detox in the steam room the next morning. At one stage when I was living in London, the gym was right below my building, and I joined the spinning class with an instructor who attempted to break world records. You can imagine the intensity he expected from us. It always surprised my colleagues and friends that I could be up and at it after a night out with minimal sleep. I am blessed with the superpower to function on little sleep. I also believe that without my workout regime, I would not have done as well in sustaining my long-term stamina doing NBS so efficiently. I was often asked what I was 'on' to keep me going, to which I could respond with a wry smile in all honesty,

"Nothing, mate. Just a good gym workout and thirty minutes in the steam room at five every morning."

I never succumbed to the temptation of experimenting with drugs or any chemical substances, for which I am eternally grateful. I hate to think what would have happened to me knowing that I don't do anything in half measures.

Go big or go home, I say!

Making friends and nurturing friendships went up a notch because I met so many new people. Okay, so this is excessive, and it's not always about quantity over quality, but there were days when I had up to eight back-to-back meetings. Most of those short meetings resulted in follow-up appointments and extended lunches. The lunches weren't a waste of time either, because amongst the business talk was a lot of *not-so-small talk*, getting to know each other and connecting at a deeper level. I was not afraid to let people see who I was, so the real Bobby Rakhit showed up at meetings and drew out the 'real client' sitting opposite me as we got to know each other. The trust created formed the glue of the solid relationships. I had some good laughs with my wingman when he complained about a client's dreary demeanour, to which I responded with a list of stuff I had learned about them or found interesting as we connected at a deeper level than most people do. I never let an

opportunity pass to get to know someone a little better, and it paid off more than I could have imagined.

I took Cindy Lauper's song title, "*Girls Just Wanna Have Fun,*" as an indictment on men being boring. Men also wanna have fun, so I planned meetings out of the client's office rather than going to their office or having them over to mine. If possible, I made it close to their office to make it easier for them to get there and be more relaxed. My modus operandi created a relaxed, friendly atmosphere. I had a few favourite spots where I knew the staff well, and they complemented my intensity with excellent service. The focus was on entertaining the client rather than mind-numbing them to death. No topics were barred, and fun was on the agenda.

I was aware that others were wooing the same clients as me. So with this in mind, I focused the second part of my planning on the brand. I ensured that the client remembered our meetings because of my unique approach to presenting myself and the brand. I became synonymous with JCF and the media. When people heard the name Bobby Rakhit, they automatically thought of JCF. When they heard JCF, they thought of Bobby Rakhit: fun, relaxed meetings, plus knowing that we (JCF and I) could solve their problems.

WORK HARD, PLAY HARD – WHAT MADE ME SUCCESSFUL

A typical day in my NBS life ....

Venue: Gaucho Grill, Liverpool Road—*The* best steak restaurant in London; their biggest serving portion, 1.2kg of prime cut steak

Bonus—they allow cigar smoking!

The Client: Top management from a prominent bank

My crew: Me, two salesmen, and my head of consulting

Hors d'oeuvres, assorted

Main course: mainly steaks between 800g and 1.2kg

Dessert, assorted

Cognac, port, and cigars

More drinks and chatting about the product and a lot of 'small talk'

Dinner: more steak (two clients from another bank who have become friends join us for dinner)

After dinner and dessert, we have more wine and cigars

My phone rings (on silent): a call from the boss to find out where we are—he declines the invitation to join us doing business

Midnight—we transfer to a members-only nightclub

The evening ends as we sign a sales contract with the bank worth £500 000 (with some handwritten notations to sweeten the deal)

The next morning, I am the first one in the office after my gym session as usual and place the signed contract on the boss's desk.

Consistently signing huge sales deals resulted in healthy profits for the company and a great annual bonus for me. The job satisfaction and lifestyle I enjoyed were awesome.

Okay, so this isn't a required attribute for success in new business sales, but it makes life there a hell of a lot sweeter in the long run.

NBS – The Final Chapter

FactSet, a global player in the field of finance, bought JCF in 2003; I was now thirty years old and ready to test more of my entrepreneurial prowess in a much bigger market. I remained in my position as director of sales working for Colin. I took the new challenge on with both hands, upped my energy levels, infiltrated the top management structures, and

made a name for myself very quickly. I have used the term *taking it to a new level* possibly too many times now to keep it credible, but I must use it again when it comes to the level of my innate leadership skills nurtured from my childhood when my peers followed me as a leader of my friendship groups. In the classrooms at school, Bobby always stood out from the crowd and was never afraid to take the lead. At my first and every subsequent job, I took on leadership roles. When NBS with JCF presented me with leadership opportunities, I volunteered to teach the young staff to prepare them for their chartered financial analyst (CFA) exams. Teaching and leadership are two of my passions. FactSet opened the opportunities, with Colin's backing, for me to grow my empire across continents. Between 2003 and 2012, I opened offices in Dubai, India, and Hong Kong and expanded the Middle East, Africa, and Asian markets.

My FactSet walk was more of a climb when it came to the corporate ladder. My division grew year on year, every year, and produced unmatched sales across the company. It was difficult for management to keep my salary confidential, and it led to much disgruntled discussion between the directors who earned less than me. Leadership was never a conscious decision at a fixed point in time; it was a gradual process of easing into my purpose on planet Earth. I was meant to lead and have an influence on the world. When I taught my staff in my national offices how I wanted them to do their jobs, I showed them by example the excellence that I expected from them and revealed their potential to do the same. As before, the FactSet staff respected me, not only *my* staff but globally. I had requests from people to come and work for me as I continued the *work hard, play harder* ethos which elicited outstanding performance and was appropriately rewarded. My staff were all highly motivated. When I left FactSet, there was a string of unhappy staff all asking me not to leave. Several of them left FactSet shortly after I did, and some now work for me in various of my businesses.

Enter Bobby Rakhit – Business owner, entrepreneur, FuM© architect

My ten-year walk with JCF/FactSet ended after countless good single malt whisky and hand-rolled Havanas celebrating big deals worth mega dollars. The job with Colin came wrapped up with a red ribbon tied in a big bow. I loved it, had tons of fun doing it, and made a giant success of it.

What goes up must come down!

All good things end, and NBS was a good thing for me that set me up in the confident position to step out and do business for myself, relying on my entrepreneurial skills to make a success. My tenure with FactSet drew to a natural end as my strong desire to branch out grew in tandem with my skills. There were possibilities of other jobs with good prospects, but that would mean working for a boss and stunting my growth as an entrepreneur, a person, and an FuM© thinker. I had outgrown the corporate world with its fickle promise of taking care of me. Despite creating a substantial business for FactSet and injecting significant impact into their growth, I was still just an employee, and all employees are dispensable.

Everything begins with a thought

I have an active mind, and thoughts run through it like the London underground trains. I am not consciously aware of all of them, but my unconscious mind, as I have learned from neuroscientists, never sleeps. It knows every thought and stores the significant ones in memory for later recall. FuM© was one such thought that ran through the station fifteen years ago without stopping long enough to be labelled. But it was stored in my memory to be recalled several times in the decisions I made from that first brief notion.

I believe that my positive energy continually combines with my thoughts. Energy, which the same scientists say, is transferred, never lost. So by the time I left FactSet, I had built a contact base of over five thousand 'C' level contacts covering Africa, Asia, and the Middle East. Constructed with the future in mind, my network was a building block in the solid foundation I could rely on when I established my own enterprise. It was something I steadily maintained by keeping regular contact. Because of the strong entrepreneurial passion running through my veins, I spent the years in corporate employment making a point of creating the Bobby Rakhit brand. Consequently, my thoughts have subconsciously always included the entrepreneurial vision just like FuM©. My close involvement in each deal created a following and laid down a solid track record that I could leverage in any future career, including going solo.

My passion for learning was something that stood with me from the day my uncle gave me a set of encyclopaedias for my tenth birthday in Halifax. It launched me into a world of information I wanted to turn into knowledge that inspired me to pursue more throughout my school career, college, and university. I accumulated several degrees and certificates with several academic accolades. I never restricted my appetite for knowledge to formal education either. I was a sponge soaking up experience and skills, then teaching others.

The personal well-maintained library of information I had to draw from put me in the perfect position to do two important things now that I was on my own. I could confidently take calculated risks by applying my knowledge across various business disciplines. Added to this was my ability, as my peers put it, of being able to sell ice to a Yupik, AKA Eskimo, which I recently heard was a derogatory term imposed by non-indigenous people.

I sold my bike for more than my mother paid for it.

My FuM© mindset originally began, as you've read, when I invested money at the age of sixteen, and my mother couldn't believe it.

Here's an excerpt from my autobiography with a little more detail:

Not only was I going to be rich, but I also had the savvy to work out that the money I made could be increased without taking on more jobs or working harder. The hard work paid off without a doubt, but the money had to be invested to attract interest and grow my savings. The Royal Bank of Canada opened its doors and a savings account for me to take my first steps on my journey to feed my curiosity in the world of investments. I even took out a retirement plan with my first paycheque at the tender teenage time when other kids were oblivious to the fact that they were getting older or even thinking about their retirement.

My mindset was evolving when I purchased our family home, settling the mortgage for my mother with the first real cash I earned. Then the mindset of planning my retirement as a kid was eventually deconstructed and reconstructed into FuM©. I was always looking for ways to make more money. I worked multiple jobs simultaneously, twice as hard as necessary, until I learned to let money work for me. The transformation began when I was still at university and continued throughout my career to where I am today.

Needless to say, I am not the same today as I was standing in front of a group of bankers where I found myself in a classroom in my first formal job in the finance industry. Each job I had changed me in some way, but fundamentally, I was always focused on amassing as much wealth as possible.

FuM© only came into the picture once I was a business owner and included my entrepreneurial skills into the equation, planning the growth of my wealth. Entrepreneurship would become a piece of the puzzle that fitted perfectly into the culture. It helped me flesh out my thinking about creating passive income streams and has evolved, keeping me consistently on the lookout for new investment opportunities.

All the subsequent investing and creating passive income streams became the basis of my eventual FuM© strategy, which turbo-boosted during my time at JCF/FactSet. As I progressed in the transformation process, I headed up a separate division of FactSet, which I thought was approaching a plateau. Before an offer of a great job, I could not say *"F$CK YOU MONEY"* to any that came along.

Not all bad, as it was just what I needed to nudge me into finally transforming into a full-blown entrepreneur. The new mindset embraced the well-being of myself and my family and removed the insatiable greed and obsolete security of my retirement schemes. My time with JCF and eventually heading up a separate division at FactSet put me in a financial position with a secure enough buffer to allow me to resign and go on my own.

I was on my way!

MY WALK CONTINUES

It is 2012, and I am 39 years old. I was wrong about my life slowing down after my sabbatical. Twenty years crammed into the last ten, and I do not regret one second. I am finally saddling up my entrepreneurial steed to go solo into full-on independence for the Rakhit family, taking on the responsibility without a hint of compromise. Doing it for myself is taking me to another level of accountability compared to having the backing of a large corporate company where I operated as an internal entrepreneur.

Here we go again with *'taking things to the next level'*. My passion for doing business, taking on a new challenge, making a success and having fun doing it, although different from the *Wolf of Wall Street* world I lived in New York, is taking on a completely new identity as the intensity grows. I am maturing.

A TOTALLY NEW WALK

My family's security was paramount; all of our futures were at stake. The steps I would take from the beginning were critical. I immediately constructed a solid foundation by securing permanent residency in Dubai for my family. I followed that up by purchasing a house, finding a suitable medical insurance provider, confirming provision for my two children's ongoing education, and ensuring general security and financial stability. All the factors needed to ensure a seamless transition from perceived 'corporate security', plus my wedding vows, were in place.

Having the peace of mind knowing that my family's future was secure, I moved on to set up a company under the name Inside Consulting FZE.

ACTION

I started with the creation of a credible advisory board made up of people I knew and trusted, most of whom are still with me today. The business needed a website to facilitate online client communication and expose my brand in a way that matched my credibility in the marketplace.

The company profile uses the Golden Triangle of Asia on top, Africa on the bottom left, and the Middle East at the bottom right as its base. I set up a family office to oversee all of my investment operations and ensure the continuity of my legacy. I made the definite decision that all of my future business dealings would be on a contractual or partner agreement basis. I was never going to be employed by a company again. I was my own boss.

With the Free Zone Enterprise (FZE) company registered, I have to decide what the business activities will be.

Number one: It will be the conduit for FuM©.

Number two: I must have more than one income stream to ensure a consistent flow of revenue to provide the security I prioritised for my family and my future.

Number three: I must have a sustainable company.

FACT

Roughly 80 percent of new businesses survive past their first year of operation. However, only around half of all new businesses exist after five years, and only one-third make it past their tenth anniversary. These statistics have been remarkably consistent through the years, even during major economic downturns. The good news is that survival rates begin to flatten out after several years of operation. The longer a business lasts, the more likely it is to last even longer.

I consider my options based on my skills, my track record, my network and the opportunities in the marketplace. My mindset is ring-fenced with the modus operandi of taking a calculated risk. Every decision I make will pass through that filter. The business or businesses I choose need to have the three requisites of being unique, profitable, and sustainable. Ultimately, these active sources of income need to convert into my sustainable FuM©.

Everything begins with a thought, and I remember that over the years, I came across the difficulties individuals and companies faced trying to raise capital. When I worked at Deloitte in Mergers and Acquisitions, I gained in-depth knowledge of the process, more than simply raising capital. I assessed a company's investment viability. I have a global network putting me in a great position to match capital requirements with several providers. I can become a conduit for companies trying to raise capital from abroad. I put my feelers out in the local Middle East market and get some quick bites. One such opportunity is funding Rare Earth projects that can provide significant economic value for a particular country. This is perfect because many Middle Eastern countries' long-term vision is to become less dependent on oil exports.

It's an opportunity with the potential to create a gravy train that will rapidly set Inside Consulting FZE up as a serious player in the capital markets. The substantial monthly retainer will also meet my immediate financial needs.

Unfortunately, it turns out to be a well that runs dry. But it taught me a good life lesson: *Nothing is as easy as it seems.* It did, however, set up the infrastructure for better vetted future deals. Deals that turned into substantial rewards that contributed significantly to building up my passive income.

The first pillar of the business is decided.

Closing deals is my forte, especially in the Fintech business. The years spent in investment banking and technology companies, where I rubbed shoulders with numerous CTOs and COOs of these financial firms, put me in a privileged position. These people make purchasing decisions. My intimate knowledge of solving complex problems and understanding their technology gaps gives me an unprecedented advantage. I connect with some contacts in the field. One of them puts me in touch with a Dutch-based fintech firm that addresses some of these gaps. To my benefit, they also hit my 'Goldilocks' area. A growing firm with a well-established client base in several European banks but no presence in the East or African markets.

Perfect!

They offer me a partnership agreement, the start of my fintech business.

The second pillar is *decided.*

Finally, I know I can find a way of making money by feeding my passion for sharing my knowledge through formally educating young people who want to get into the finance industry. I approach several high-level educational institutions in Dubai, leveraging my previous experience as a guest lecturer in several universities in the UK. I get a call from SP Jain School of Global Management's Executive MBA (EMBA) program.

They offer me a slot to teach portfolio management in Dubai. It is an opportunity to work with the World's Top 100 (81st) and Asia-Pacific's Top 10 (7th) by Ivy Exec (USA) EMBA Rankings, making it one of the world's best EMBA programs.

The third pillar is decided.

It feels like an unnecessary suit of heavy armour has been removed from my shoulders. I can breathe my own air, not filtered through a corporate mask. I am Muhammad Ali, as light as a butterfly dancing around the ring, ready to sting like a bee. I am well prepared with all the attributes and skills to make every punch count. My eyes are open, and my naivety is safely locked away to avoid any nasty surprises. All the years of sparring are behind me as the bell rings for my first professional bout.

Advanced Entrepreneurship

This was it: All the training was about to be put to the test. This was the real deal, and I was up for it. As I realised long ago, I am a born entrepreneur. But that doesn't mean I had everything I required for the job. Some skills and attributes were innate, others had been cultivated, and the rest were learned as required to complete the package.

Passion for Life and People

My passion was never in short supply. I often smile at and talk to myself in the mirror in the morning when I am starting my day to get me going. It is a powerful attribute proportionate to my success. My energy and passion attract people to me like bees to honey. It generates contagious energy that syncs with the universal positive energy flowing around us.

Just watch the spectators at a football match. The passion and energy could launch a rocket ship. Or a five-year-old eating ice cream. Better still, try and get their attention off the ice cream.

It's almost impossible.

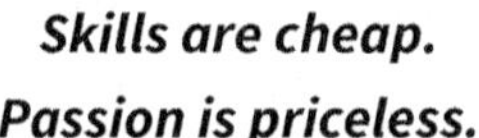

Skills are cheap.
Passion is priceless.

Gary Vaynerchuk

Physiologically, passion creates excitement and releases cocktail doses of oxytocin, endorphins, serotonin, adrenaline, and dopamine into the bloodstream, creating an atmosphere for positive conversations. I love watching a person's face light up and enjoy a conversation when they sense my passion for engaging with them on a personal level. They can't help but catch it too.

As an entrepreneur and an employer, I find that the strength of my teams stems from intimate connection and genuine interest in their lives.

And as an entrepreneur connecting with clients, I find that putting connection ahead of business results in much better outcomes.

Non-judgemental

I genuinely love people with a passion. I never contradict myself like some people I hear saying they love people and refute themselves with their actions when they gossip and pass judgement. It's often just a cliché used to impress the listener. As ancient wisdom warns us, I separate my ego from my identity and nurture relationships with family, socially, or professionals with the same outlook. I do not judge or try to fit people into my box of acceptance. A non-judgemental attitude is a fundamental aspect of my entrepreneurial walk as anything that forms part of the FuM© philosophy. I am free of pre-conditioned thinking and judgementalism. People are so interesting when I give them a chance to have a word. I find that most conversations I hear are more about one dominant person giving their point of view and never asking for anyone else's opinion. In *my* opinion, that stems from personal insecurity. It's difficult for a lot of people to listen. I love to listen to other people's

stories they share eagerly, given a non-judgemental chance. Once you have that connection, the conversations get richer.

Self-Confidence

It's not who you are that holds you back.
It's who you think you're not.

Eric Thomas, motivational speaker

My time at school, shovelling snow, college, university, Wall Street, and NBS created a three-legged platform for me of self-esteem, self-worth and self-love. All three cooperated in unison for me to eventually function self-confidently as an entrepreneur, without which I would have wobbled and perhaps crumbled. But I survived to tell you that I came out in one piece with all three pillars standing steady and my self-confidence exactly where I needed it to perform with excellence. There was no guarantee that I would make it, simply based on my history. The test of entrepreneurial self-confidence is severe.

Many conversations I have had over the years with friends and colleagues revealed a deep-seated resistance to facing their reflection in the mirror. Few of them gazed into the eyes looking back at them. It can be a very uncomfortable experience when you do it for the first time. It is easy to comb your hair, shave your beard, or check your makeup without intentionally connecting with the person *behind* the reflection.

Ancient wisdom says that some people hear wise words but disregard them like a person who looks in a mirror and immediately forgets what they look like.

Modern wisdom says that poor self-esteem is one of the main reasons we do not like to look at ourselves in the mirror. I find this to be true of people who don't look me in the eye. Sadly, millions of humans cannot face their reflections in the mirror.

Our self-esteem begins taking shape in childhood, influenced by parents, siblings, teachers, friends, and the media. If the input is negative, it can make you feel despondent, thinking you're a failure. The negative messages we receive growing up are the ones that resonate louder than the positive ones. They dilute the 'you are good enough' messages no matter how many you receive.

Returning from my six-month sabbatical, I experienced an epiphany highlighting a self-worth issue I was unaware of. Before my life-changing adventure, I never struggled with my self-esteem and spent little time pondering the subject.

By the time I flew the coop into the big, wide world, the gift of positive self-confidence had been solidly inculcated into me by my mother, my grandfather, and my teachers. I learned to love and believe in myself. A priceless, powerful gift that paid huge dividends when I kept it safely in check from inflating my ego. My self-confidence got me through my first days at junior school when being in an ethnic minority tested it to the limit. Most of the kids were mates from the neighbourhood, so they ganged up and put me in a 'box' where they could ridicule me verbally and assault me physically by pushing my head down a toilet bowl. I had to make quick decisions so my healthy self-confidence could rebuff the attack. If I'd crumbled, I would have been scarred for life, believing the negative message that I was not good enough. Or I could rely on my self-confidence and hold my head up high, letting my intellect and athletic skills on the sports field speak for me. I chose the latter and ended my school career at the top of the honour roll with an 'A' average and numerous sporting awards. Of course, there were very positive messages from many of my teachers and later from my tertiary educators.

But Wall Street was the real self-confidence boot camp. It began when Richard Bilotti allowed me to join his world-leading research team. After my final interview, he shoved a stack of books in my hands, told me to go home, read them, and come back in a week to start writing a book with him. I didn't get much sleep ploughing through them. Then before I finished reading, he called me back into the office and told me I had the job and to get started. A job that not only included writing the book, it ran concurrently with company orientation, learning how to do research, *plus* full-on daily participation in team operations.

Being shoved into an automatic washing machine and put on the full wash and spin cycle is not fun. For most humans, sleep deprivation means being unable to go back to sleep quickly after a bad dream. Morgan Stanley taught me that sleep deprivation was not sleeping for seventy-two hours straight to complete a research assignment.

Where school, college, and university sometimes tested my self-belief to the point of self-doubt, Wall Street repeatedly affirmed my self-belief. Going from university, first to Deloitte Touche, then to Wall Street's seventy-two-hour shifts without shutting an eye, was never on my list of things to do before I die. I now know that I *can* do it. Co-authoring a book on a subject that I had been given one week to digest was not on my list of desired competencies until I did it. The achievement of becoming a research-team leader on Wall Street at Morgan Stanley was as farfetched as becoming a boy scout patrol leader in my youth; I was never a boy scout. From my first gig teaching mathematics to young schoolkids to teaching bankers about Canadian Securities gave me enough chutzpah to volunteer my services to teach CFA prep (an extremely tough accreditation) to my peers.

Then returning from my sabbatical, a fault line in my self-esteem appeared one morning as I looked into the mirror, shaving my stubble. Looking into my eyes, I saw the authentic Bobby Rakhit for the first time in my life. I looked deep into my soul and found the core of who I am, not just a reflection staring back at me. It was eerie at first, then a spontaneous smile pulled at my lips, my eyes narrowed, and I chuckled to myself. It felt strange, but the warm glow that flowed through my body reassured my sanity. My thoughts relayed the message that the mask of self-confidence I wore to that point was a neatly painted façade. In that instant, I stepped out from behind it and saw myself for who I was. It was the real Bobby Rakhit.

I *loved* who I saw.

That self-actualising experience gave me the self-confidence that spurred my success in new business sales with complete confidence. The same thing happened when I took the plunge into independent entrepreneurship, just more so.

ARROGANCE VS HUMILITY

Many of Rambo's traits stuck with me, especially the way he balanced the fine line between arrogance and humility in his life. It was another lesson confirmed by the ancient wisdom incorporated into FuM© of detaching ego from significance.

Too much humility makes you a floor mat. Too much arrogance makes you an @rsehole!

The good news from psychologists is that damaged self-esteem is repairable. There is no quick-fix solution, though, because of the deep-seated damage corroded by the narrative of life.

> ***"I have often wondered how it is everyone loves himself more than the rest of men, yet sets less value on his own opinions of himself than the opinions of others."***
>
> *Marcus Aurelius – Second century Roman Emperor*

As Marcus Aurelius puts it:

Renowned self-help, spiritual author, and motivational speaker Wayne Dyer has a lot to say about self-actualisation and sums it up with this great quote:

> Self-actualized people are independent of the good opinion of others.
>
> — *Wayne Dyer* —

Self-Actualization

My first *'mirror experience'* when I returned from my HSBC-sponsored sabbatical was me becoming a self-actualized person. I accepted myself and others unconditionally just as they are. I have no hang-ups and can enjoy myself living a guilt-free life. The beauty of a self-actualized person lies in the ability to embrace other people for who they are as well.

Think self-acceptance—don't waste time on negative self-talk.

Self-belief is the fruit of self-confidence and self-actualisation, the fruit of authentic self-revelation. It is one thing to have a healthy self-confidence, but to fully believe in yourself, you need to love yourself.

Without a positive self-esteem, self-belief, self-actualisation and a measure of over-confidence I would never make it as an entrepreneur.

Perfectionism

Attempting to avoid failure at all costs by doing it perfectly when I started my own business cost me dearly. I planned, prepared, deliberated, and executed my activities with finite precision, leaving no 'T' uncrossed or 'I' un-dotted. It drained my energy to the point of exhaustion and slowed me down, wasting my time. Then it occurred to me that I was being too rigid in expecting certainty in all of the key outcomes in the businesses. I hit pause, took a deep breath, and decided that entrepreneurship was not simply a case of 1 + 1 = 2 as I was trying to force it to be. Sometimes 1 + 1 = 1.5 or even zero, so I made the change, and it worked. Accepting a 'change is inevitable' mindset has kept me sane and ended successfully every time. It put an end to my procrastination and the distraction of trying to reach the perfection that was costing me sleepless nights and draining my energy.

I still strived for perfection, but I wasn't bogged down by it.

My perfectionism was leading to procrastination. Procrastination was leading to indecision. Indecision was leading to failure. Failure was leading to disappointment. Disappointment was leading to depression.

I read an article on psychology that said our most dominant character trait could be our worst enemy if we didn't keep it in check. It helped me stop trying to plan business perfectly. FuM©, without perfectly predictable outcomes and some variables, made me more relaxed and flexible without losing the plot.

Perfectionism has become my ally, not my enemy.

Creativity

Changing lanes from NBS into my own businesses created the platform to engage the creativity described in *My walk continued. But* the ultimate endorsement of it is the construction of FuM©. In case you were in doubt, I believe that FuM© is a unique idea creatively conceived, incubated, and birthed as I grew accustomed to the environment I found myself in.

Environment

When I walked into full-blown entrepreneurship for the first time, it challenged my understanding and perception enough to create my own reality in an unfamiliar environment. I soon got to know the lay of the

land, which was daunting and exciting. I was not new to environmental influences on my life. The Bobby Rakhit writing this book, heading up multiple business interests, creating FuM© culture, and leaving a legacy did not pop out of a party cake. If I had never landed up in a rat-hole hotel having to fake my way through school pretending to be okay, without a father to mentor me, learning to cope on my own with a single mother, I would not be the person I am today. I had options and choices to make. So many people I know who are not doing well in life live in a blame bubble, making excuses for their lot in life. A good friend who counsels drug addicts and alcoholics tells me that one of the main reasons people end up self-medicating with drugs and alcohol is to stop feeling sorry for themselves. They blame everything and everyone but themselves for their situation. I've also heard stories of criminals who blame their poor decisions on their childhood environment. Then I think of two brothers with abusive alcoholic parents. One becomes an alcoholic, while the other is a non-drinking, upright, successful businessman.

I'm not saying that people don't land up in dire straits through no fault of their own. I am saying that we all have a choice to make in how we handle the circumstances.

I could have ended up staying in a drug rehab like the house my mother and I lived in for a while after the rat's nest hotel. She managed through a friend to get a job there while she looked for the permanent job that got us out of the situation my father left us in. I chose to take responsibility for myself and ended up writing this book. Thankfully, my mother got a permanent job, worked her guts out, and got us into a better environment in a healthy suburban community, albeit without a father to guide me. In hindsight, it was much better for my mother and me without my father. I made up my mind:

I was never going to be poor. I would make sure I was rich! I was going to get a job on Wall Street.

That disparate situation created a hunger in me to survive and succeed. I am proud not to have felt entitled like most kids today who believe that the world owes them something. It owes them nothing.

The environment I grew up in moulded me into an independent, capable adult making it possible for me to pull off an unscripted assignment that began on May 25th, 2020, when my mother passed away unexpectedly in Canada. With no military training besides the Rambo movies, I left Dubai at the height of the COVID-19 global pandemic within nine days of her death. The world was locked down, with inter-continental travel restrictions. I not only got to Canada to bury my mother, but I packed up and sold her household contents, plus the house. I also tied up the financial implications of her failure to make out a will. All while seeing to the needs of my frail, grieving, 98-year-old grandmother. I miraculously arranged for her immigration to return to Dubai with me. Dubai does not allow elderly immigration. If that wasn't enough, she fell and broke both wrists a few weeks before we were to fly. They miraculously healed in time too.

0 STOP

Think about that. Medical history tells us that healthy bones take three to six months to heal, never mind an old lady's fragile bones. The X-rays showed complete healing!

Δ PLAY

Embedded within this military exercise was the final manoeuvre to get from Montréal to Toronto with my grandmother, restricted to a wheelchair. We did it, and kudos to her, she was a great traveller and still lives with us, soon to reach the 100-year milestone. It took me 82 days from the time I left on May 9th until my return with Granny in her wheelchair. An assignment I don't think I could have done without the history of my character-building childhood environment.

Tenacity, Perseverance, Positivity

These were best modelled for me by my mother and cultivated into positivity by me. She showed relentless tenacity and perseverance from the day my father left us in the lurch and never stopped until I received the call that no child wishes to get. I still miss her, but I live the legacy of the example she set. I applied these traits to my studies, sport, work, and making money. It's still a case of full throttle or not worth doing, making plans, thinking on my feet, competing with my peers, forging ahead, and running away from my past. I hate losing. I have no problem giving up personal comfort in exchange for eventual success.

I will give you an example from my childhood that makes me smile whenever I think of it. I remind my children of it when I want to teach them these traits. A piece from my autobiography when my mother and I were living in the drug rehab best describes it.

We had been staying there for some time when close to Christmas that year, Mum received divorce papers from my father which nearly crushed her. We hadn't seen him for a long time, and out of nowhere, she got this devastating news. The predicament I was in makes the memories of this time very intense as I was recovering from both my ankles being broken. The first one was broken playing basketball and the second while I was playing in the final indoor soccer championship with one ankle already broken.

"Yes, I agree, not very clever!"

It was a painful time for us both, Mum reading and re-reading the divorce papers and me with my two ankles in plaster casts having to get to the hospital myself to get crutches so I could get to school every day. It wasn't funny then, but I laugh at my stupidity now.

Imagine the scene: Mum distraught about the divorce and me sitting with my plaster-clad ankles up on a chair. I sat looking up at the night sky and noticed Orion's belt; it seemed to be saying to me that everything would

be fine, just as it had done several times before during tough times in my life. The three main stars whispering that things always happen in threes. Two broken ankles, staying in a drug house and the divorce papers. I looked at Mum and said, "Mum, don't worry, everything is going to be fine. This is probably the best thing that has happened to you. Now you can start a new life. It's a fresh start for us. I have a good feeling about this."

It was my awakening to universal positive energy and how it affects our lives. I had first-hand exposure to the power of my positive energy that has stayed with me and carries me through the troughs of life, especially as I continue my walk as an entrepreneur. Rambo and I never stay down long when we hit adversity in our lives. It sometimes takes me a day of grinding through the situation with the help of a good bottle of wine or a few whiskies and bouncing back stronger.

Don't Sweat the Small Stuff... and it's all small stuff

(by Richard Carlson)

I am sure that Richard Carlson's 1997 book is for entrepreneurs. Outside of my formal education, I experienced a lot of self-educating life lessons by reading books like this. He taught me the valuable lesson of avoiding the worries of little things that used to drive me crazy. His thoughtful and insightful language introduced ways for me to calm down amid a hurried, stress-filled life. It changed my thinking, putting things in perspective by making small daily changes and, importantly, thinking of problems as potential teachers. He gives the simple advice of remembering that when you die, your *Inbox* will not be empty and to do only one thing at a time. He puts a lot of emphasis on something I have always tried to do too: *Live in the present moment.* Now, with my ego where it belongs outside of me, I let others take praise for the achievements they attain because of my input.

Listing my most stubborn positions and attitudes helped soften them up just as he said they would. They still pop up now and again, but I

recognise them and deal with them as *small stuff*. I especially trust my intuition and live each day as if it might be my last. His gentle, supportive suggestions persuaded me to make my actions more peaceful and caring, making my life much calmer and less stressful.

We all need a little healthy stress to stay alive.

His advice helped, especially with my philosophy of putting relationships before closing a deal. My best friend Nick, the brother I never had, was the best man at my wedding. Our friendship began when he was a prospective client. He has not spent a dollar on any of my products to date. Sweating that *small issue* would have cost me a very dear friend. Many of my solid friendships began with a business meeting and are now part of a close contact list. Not sweating the small stuff of an unsigned deal eventually produced some large deals simply because they passed my name on to other people in their networks.

I can say in all honesty that drumming up leads in business is never my incentive for forming and nurturing friendships.

Ask yourself: Will it matter a year from today?

HELPFUL HINTS

Start with a never give up attitude

Listen rather than react

Lost deals are lost

Future deals are not signed yet

Work on the deal you're working on

Give it all you've got!

Life is a boat ride. Looking back cannot change the wake; you can only affect what's happening in the boat.

Education and Knowledge

Nogg's education was based on *monkey see, monkey do*. More recent education, albeit from a time when education for Egyptians and Indians included only a privileged minority. Subjects covered were morality, astrology, religious beliefs, and philosophy.

> ***If you are not willing to learn, no one can help you.***
> ***If you are determined to learn, no one can stop you.***
>
> *Zig Ziglar*

Education in the *Technological Revolution* is available to most and in many cases at no cost. FuM©'s acceptance of ancient wisdom is a classic example of the endurance and credibility of the truth. There are no restrictions to what we can learn today; it is up to the individual just how much time and energy you are prepared to spend broadening your knowledge through formal or self-education. Reading newspapers and magazine articles keeps me in touch with current circumstances to see what my competitors are up to so I can stay ahead of them. I have constantly learned from my peers, associates, and mentors to this day and am not about to stop.

Most of us don't like making mistakes, let alone admit to making them. I see them as opportunities to learn and avoid making them again. My country bumpkin upbringing caused me much embarrassment to the amusement of friends and colleagues. Besides my dress sense, I had trouble cutting a piece of steak because we could never afford it. The ragging stopped after receiving training from a seasoned steak eater. My white socks with my short-long pants raised a few eyebrows and more chuckles. There were other more serious mistakes that I won't go into, except to say I only paid the school fees once.

I shudder to think what would have become of me if my mother had not sacrificed her life to the point of leaving her homeland, India, and her supportive family to give me the opportunity to attend good schools and universities in Canada. Her strong Indian cultural heritage esteemed education more precious than rubies, so she encouraged and guided me, instilling a hunger for knowledge. I committed myself to my education from the start. First, I aced the entrance exam to get into Halifax Grammar School. Then I closed each school year off at the top of the honour roll. Dedicated to my studies, I worked hard and played harder, passionately participating in multiple sports.

Continuing in the same vein, I successfully included part-time work into the equation in my senior school career to make some money. What made it more significant was that this phase of my education was critical to gaining acceptance into a college. It required more commitment than I was used to, and I aced that too.

My diligence there allowed me to chart a course of higher learning at an excellent college where I continued to work part-time jobs and earn money. I still took part in sport and kept myself fit and healthy. It was college that set me up to obtain a university degree and a job at Abbott Laboratories that kick-started my dream to get to Wall Street.

I must add that I was blessed with a bright intellect to go with my good schooling. I relied on my smarts to get good jobs that I merged with hard work, which I learned from my mother, to reach the top position in every job I've had. My education took me out of a cycle of scarcity that could have trapped me if I'd dismissed its value.

All my jobs have required some level of learning, which I embraced and applied myself diligently to. The pile of books I was given to read at Morgan Stanley made their mark on a topic I had never heard of before. I am proud to say that the result of that compressed, pressurised education resulted in the publication of Richard Bilotti's book, which I mentioned previously.

My education never stopped after university. To use an old cliché, *you never stop learning*. Informal education is as powerful as formal.

You know by now that my dream was to work on Wall Street and make loads of money. I set my goal early and plotted a course to achieve the dream. It didn't stop when I got to Wall Street. I soon realised that I would have to continue adding to my knowledge daily to stay ahead of the pack, including more formal education. After researching the options, I decided that the chartered financial analyst route would put me in a league of highly respected global executives. Just where I wanted to be. I enrolled and successfully earned my charter; it was the toughest course I have attempted, and I was delighted to add it to my armoury.

My CFA charter has opened many doors for me. It has been a crucial contributor to my business success. The studying I put in has been worth the effort and sacrifice when I see the rewards from my intellectual property. I am proud of the respect shown towards me by peers and superiors alike. Knowledge cannot be lost or taken away. It pays me back every day.

Body Language

Your body communicates as well as your mouth. Don't contradict yourself.

Allen Ruddock

A good mate of mine worked in different roles throughout his career and told me about an experience he had as a young man in his first job with a national airline. He was part of a technical training team preparing to visit Singapore to teach their airline staff how to use a computer program. It was his first proper teaching gig. The subject

was no problem for him, but the presentation turned out to be an eye-opener. He says,

We had to choose a task we could successfully teach fellow trainers to carry out within a five-minute video recording. I selected the Full-Windsor knot for neckties. My technique was flawless, and everyone enjoyed the short lesson. The crunch, however, came when the time came to critique each other's recorded videos. Most of us were diplomatic with our comments, and I received mine graciously when told I lacked enthusiasm. I was more shocked by what I saw on the video replay than by the comment. My body language totally contradicted my enthusiasm. The tone of my voice and the drop of my shoulders told a different story. My facial expression was not too bad but did not make up for the negatives. Slipping back into the auditorium during the lunch break, I watched myself again a few times.

It was a life-changing experience for which I have been forever grateful. I now carry myself with self-confidence in my being. I immediately make corrections when I catch my shoulders dropping or my voice losing its friendly edge. I check my attitude, realise that I am not feeling good about myself, and find out why.

Reading body language

I had a similar experience when I was doing my MBA and had to deliver a formal presentation to the group. I was well prepared, and the delivery was on point. Afterwards, Professor Prince called me aside and complimented me on the contents and preparation but pointed out that my monotone presentation made it boring. It was one of those *education through mistakes* moments that has never since heard me deliver even a casual conversation in an uninteresting, monotone voice.

It wasn't a lack of enthusiasm about the presentation; my delivery just told a contradictory story.

Prof Prince gave me this stellar advice:

"Bobby, the secret to delivering a great presentation or having a good conversation is simply this. Be yourself."

I have always been able to read body language. I don't get it right every time, but pretty often, I am spot on. In tertiary education, I learned that body language is the most important yet least emphasised aspect of communication. I believe this to be true and apply it in my business and social life. I keep fine-tuning it during conversations, especially in first-time meetings. If a client is stiff and uneasy, I turn on some humour, crack a joke, and ease the tension. It works every time and even puts me at ease hearing the laughter. Reading the different signals helps me steer conversations in and out of negative spaces.

When my client sits with their arms folded, I know they feel threatened or protective, so I give them something to hold, like a brochure, and they lower their guard. If they lean toward me with one shoulder, I know there is a measure of aggression, so I open my shoulders and my hands towards them, creating an aura of peaceful energy.

I am alert, focused, and attentive in every encounter, so my client knows I mean business. My gift of a huge friendly smile matches my passion for life, and I use it like a weapon to create a relaxed atmosphere. I make direct eye contact to show I have nothing to hide, sure that my words and tone of voice match my body language. My mobile phone is off or on 'do not disturb'. I don't plan a reply until I fully understand what they are saying to me.

I have two ears and one mouth for a very good reason. So I can listen twice as much as I talk.

If I am unsure, I will respond with something like,

"I'm not sure I understand you correctly. You're saying..."

This way, I can understand the landscape they deal with and plan a response.

There is no *five-step* or *ten-step* formula to follow for being a great communicator, but there are some golden keys, of which body language is vital. The raw fact is that it *speaks* 70 to 93 percent of person-to-person communication.

Over and above body language, I take particular notice when I lose a deal. I try to confirm whether the client is rejecting me, the product, or the price. It helps with *not sweating the small stuff.*

If they reject me, I try a different approach to selling myself. I find that empathy helps, and I take the conversation in a more personal direction. Often the client feels unheard despite my attentive approach. I probe to find out where we are missing each other. If I have given it my best shot and still cannot connect with them, I know there is nothing more I can do.

If they reject the product, I refer them to a satisfied client and follow up once they have connected. If they still reject the product, I am satisfied that I have done everything I can and continue to be friends.

If they reject the price, I can sharpen my pencil or offer them a more affordable option. If they turn that down, I know I have done everything possible, and we remain friends.

I believe in turning enemies into friends.

The choice

I am not embarrassed to say that making a ton of money was the biggest motivator when I started work of any sort, even when I shovelled snow off driveways. It worked well for me, and I got hungrier the more money I made. Several years later, if you ask me what motivates me, I will say that FuM© has refined my motivation to live within the gambit of ancient wisdom and modern capitalism. If I were back where I started setting up my walk into entrepreneurship, I would not change a thing. So many moving parts in this perfect universe collaborated to provide me with the path to FuM©—another miracle for which I am grateful. I played my role as scripted and poured my positive energy into the mix.

Enough of *My Walk*, now it's about *yours.*

It's time for you to make a choice that will change your life forever.

In an interesting article I read recently, they say the process for school leavers choosing a career varies from subject choice need to follow the desired direction to hearsay and peer pressure with little forethought. Think about the last gadget, car, or appliance you bought and how much research you did on the Interweb, asked friends, or checked it out in the shop before you bought it. Compare that to how much research you did to choose your career. The choice is not a buffet where you can taste a little of each dish to decide if you like it.

Barbara is a twenty-two-year-old humanities student who decided on her career based on one paragraph she read in a civics textbook at senior school. It led to her exploring more about fundamental rights with her teachers, classmates and more literature on the subject. She

felt a surge of energy each time she broached the subject and developed a clear understanding and insight into the complexities. During her school breaks, she volunteered her services at a local refugee shelter and felt an even stronger surge of energy. It never bothered her that her friends were spending their time going to movies, vacationing with their parents, and relaxing, while she worked. It inspired her because she thrived on making a difference in the refugees' lives. When it came time to choose subjects for her final years of school, she knew the requirements to follow a career in law and was well on her way to doing exactly that. Barbara's passion was so contagious that her younger brother joined her at the refugee shelter, but his interest in electronics directed him into computer studies. When asked about his school breaks with her, he says he would not change it for anything because he enjoyed being with his sister and seeing her come alive.

Barbara didn't have to do extensive research into the career prospects to know what she wanted to do. She found her purpose, which was her passion for people for whom she could make a difference.

Joshua was not as fortunate. He took up engineering studies because his parents discouraged him from pursuing his love for history. They pressured him into the perception that engineering is a more prestigious career than something like history, a decision Joshua regrets daily. He feels trapped because of parental pressure. Asked if he would consider changing, Joshua still hangs on to the fear of letting his parents down.

I imagine Barbara naturally walking into FuM© culture when she hears about it. I would not like to think what Joshua's life will look like fifteen to twenty years from now, gritting his teeth, longing to retire and get out of the engineering job. I'm also not sure if he will rekindle his passion for history to at least enjoy some of that time.

Passion can die if it is not nurtured and enjoyed.

Whatever choice you make to begin your walk to FuM© starts with unbridled passion. Your traits, skills, and attributes will follow and flourish. If it needs an outgoing personality, you will adapt if you are a little reserved. If it's a killer instinct, it will bring that out in you. Your passion will motivate your hunger to succeed, and you will become an expert at what you do. Your purpose will drive the energy you have for the career you pursue.

If you are working on your dream career, you are one of the 45 percent of people satisfied with their choice. You only need to make the FuM© choice and get going.

If you are one of the remaining 55 percent, the world is your oyster, presenting you with a delightful choice to join the other 45 percent and boost the percentage by joining the walk to FuM©.

Wayne Dyer says you should spend the last five minutes before dropping off to sleep imagining a goal you set for your future, be it short-term or long-term. Don't be scared to dream and dream big. You will see it when you believe it.

> ***"If you don't know where you are going, any road will take you there."***
>
> *Lewis Carroll - English author*

In this article of 1 July, 2022 in *New Trader U*, Steve Burns gives us some insight into current money mindset (edited by me).

> ***"Vision without action is merely a dream. Action without vision just passes the time. Vision with action can change the world."***
>
> *Joel Barker - Independent scholar and futurist*

For most people being rich or being poor starts with a mindset. Where you begin in life is possibly defined by fate, where you eventually end up is primarily based on providence, your thoughts, beliefs, and mindset. How your circumstances, relationships, and finances trend are due to your actions, and the root of most actions are based on how you think. So let us look into the different mindsets of growing wealth and struggling with personal finances by starting with the mindset of the wealthy.

The Ramsey Solutions survey of over 10,000 millionaires found that 79 percent of them never received any inheritance. One in three Americans who receive money through an inheritance blow it and don't invest a dollar of it. Similarly, 70 percent of lottery winners whether they win $500 million or $1 million lose or spend it all within five years or less.

Many people born into humble situations go on to build wealth and conversely, wealthy children that squander their opportunities end up broke. Do not despair, however; regardless of where you find yourself, you can redirect your thinking into a new path and create a healthy, wealthy money mindset. The healthy, wealthy mindset thinks about creating, building, and compounding assets. Wealthy people create more than they consume and love their work more than their vacations and buying stuff. They build wealth by managing their finances, investment portfolios, real estate holdings, business, or cash-producing assets. The wealthy mindset incorporates the calculated risk mentality concerning the return on capital risk versus reward. It is typically an entrepreneurial mindset of creating products, services, investments, businesses, and jobs for others. They are creative and turn their ideas into reality to produce value. Switching to the unhealthy money mindset, they found that this type of person, surrounded by opportunities, will ignore them because they have a poverty mindset. Their negative energy stems from victimhood, jealousy, and blaming fate for dealing them a low blow. Closed-mindedness is the primary sign of an unhealthy money mindset.

Conversion of this mindset takes the effort of seeing abundance instead of lack to begin. To stop going with the flow that poverty is your lot in life.

Money Wisdom

Money is a means to an end, not the meaning of life.

It is not tough to make money.

Working a job is only one way of making money.

Money is easy to keep up with but tough to catch up with; don't spend what you don't have.

Money is a good servant but a terrible master.

FuM© mindset will tell you:

Value your money, time, and energy—they are yours to spend wisely.

Convert earned income into assets by investing.

Spend more time creating wealth (passive income) than consuming your capital.

Spend money assets with positive cash flow rather depreciating your assets.

Learn to create, buy, or sell cash flowing assets.

Follow your passion and work energy—do what you love, and gamify your walk.

Write down your short- and long-term goals in every area of your life.

Believe setbacks are only temporary as you look for another path.

Wealth creation starts with your thoughts and builds through working smart and hard to reach your FuM© vision.

A word of advice on whatever you decide, especially if it is independent entrepreneurship. Make sure your *yes* is *yes* and your *no* is *no*—no bullsh$t. The truth is what matters. If you profess to have a required skill that you don't possess, it will be exposed, and you will come off second best. Always show up as you, not who you think you should be or who *you* think others think you should be.

Caroline is a fifty-year-old friend of mine who recently quit her day job to take on a role as a personal coach. Nothing surprising until I tell you that she is a medical doctor who has worked in a state hospital in Australia for the past twenty years. As a young child, Caroline dressed up in her homemade nurse outfit with a plastic stethoscope around her neck. Her dolls, teddy bears, and fluffy animal toys were tended to with loving care, keeping them healthy. She diligently took her mother's temperature with her drinking straw thermometer and recorded her heart rate every morning after breakfast before doing the ward rounds to all of her *patients*. One morning while she measured her mother's vital signs, she announced that she was no longer a nurse, but had progressed to being a doctor. Her mother silently hoped it was not a surgical doctor.

Twenty-five years on, Caroline's daily routine begins as it has for the past ten years, with a gym workout at 5:00 a.m. seven days a week. Her workday gets going at 7:00 a.m. with a genuine stethoscope around her neck and an electronic machine constantly measuring her patients' vital signs. Her repetitive seven days a week cycle ends after the final ward rounds at 7:00 p.m. Caroline and I had a chat a few months ago, and she said that she was tired of her seven days a week doctor lifestyle and couldn't wait to retire in ten years to kick back and do absolutely nothing except enjoy herself travelling the world. I introduced her to the concept of FuM©, but she was not sure it was something she was interested in and preferred the option of living in retirement off her pension payout. I sensed a lack of energy and resentment towards what used to be her passion for healing sick people. I suggested some time off, but she said she could not afford to leave the hospital for more than a day or two. I said she could not afford to spend another day in the hospital, heading for burnout and a forced medical break.

She took four of the eight-week quota of leave owing to her and went to the Solomon Islands to scuba dive for the first time in fifteen years. It took her two weeks to unwind before she could relax and enjoy the break. As she lay sunbathing one afternoon after a morning's diving, Caroline felt the urge to take a walk along the beach. Not far into the walk, she came across a group of what looked like sun worshippers sitting crossed-legged with upturned hands resting on their knees and closed eyes. A suntanned bare-chested man sitting in the same posture sat facing them. She couldn't get the picture out of her mind of how serene they all looked. She wanted some of that serenity. Walking back, Caroline passed the group again, standing under the shade of the nearby palm trees, chatting and sipping drinks from fresh coconut shells. The bare-chested man was standing to one side, talking on his mobile phone. Taking him to be the leader, she waited until he ended the call and approached him.

That encounter turned out to be the fork in Caroline's path to get her out of the dreary rut of a life and onto a two-week course learning from the bare-chested man how to be a yoga instructor. She resigned from the hospital the day she returned to Australia and called me to tell me that she had found her calling for the second part of her life. She asked me to assist her with investment advice to create passive income and set up her FuM© goals, which she said must include at least one trip abroad every year to satisfy her wanderlust.

And here's the really interesting part of Caroline's story. While she was working at the hospital, she frequently dealt with young unmarried women who wanted to give their newborn babies up for adoption because they could not take care of them, and the fathers had abdicated

all responsibility. Caroline was planning to open what she called a 'baby home' to take care of the babies while they waited for the adoption process to be finalised, which apparently could take up to six months.

Her passion growing up went from nursing to doctoring her toys and her mother to working seven days a week going through the motions waiting for retirement in ten years. Today she has a yoga studio teaching people how to reach a state of well-being. In her spare time, she will continue feeding her passion for medicine by assisting small humans while they wait to begin life in a stable home. She also told me that she talks to her yoga crew about the option of FuM©. Caroline has become an FuM© evangelist.

Magic Johnson, another hero of mine, is a legend who rose from humble beginnings, influenced by Earvin Johnson Sr. Earvin Jr. often helped his father with his after-hours job collecting garbage. He had six siblings and three half-siblings from his father's first marriage. He knew about poverty and sharing space with nine siblings, plus Mom and Dad. He inherited his athletic genes from his father, who played high school basketball for the state of Mississippi.

Earvin started thinking about a basketball career in the eighth grade at the predominantly white Everett High School, where he suffered continual racist abuse. He was unhappy there because he preferred Sexton, a predominantly Black school. His white teammates refused to pass the ball to him and ignored him at practices. He somehow avoided getting into any altercations and formed a group of Black players that respected him as a leader. In his words taken from Wikipedia, Johnson has this to say about that time:

As I look back on it today, I see the whole picture very differently. It's true that I hated missing out on Sexton. And the first few months, I was miserable at Everett. But being bussed to Everett turned out to be one of the best things that ever happened to me. It got me out of my own little world and taught me how to understand white people, how to communicate and deal with them.

He earned the name Magic at 15 as a sophomore when he recorded a triple-double of 36 points, 18 rebounds, and 16 assists. He closed out his school playing years on a high, leading his team to a 27 to 1 loss record and averaging 28.8 points and 16.8 rebounds per game. He continued to make a name for himself through his Michigan State College days when he was looking at a career in television commentating as opposed to a professional basketball career. Thankfully, he changed his mind, accepted the draft into the LA Lakers in 1979, and never looked back. In 1996, seventeen years later, he earned $365,000 a game. Magic Johnson, the legend, played his final exhibition match in 2002 at the ripe old age of forty-three. They won by 104 to 85, with Magic scoring 12 points, ten assists, and ten rebounds.

His life story would take more than the pages of this book, so I will rely on Wikipedia to assist with a summary of his career, which has not been without some difficult times.

Wikipedia

Since his retirement, Johnson has been an advocate for HIV/AIDS prevention and safe sex, as well as an entrepreneur, philanthropist, broadcaster, and motivational speaker. His public announcement of his HIV-positive status in 1991 helped dispel the stereotype widely held that HIV was a "gay disease" that excluded heterosexuals. He received wide commendation for making this brave announcement.

Named by Ebony *magazine as one of America's most influential Black business executives in 2009, Johnson has many business interests and was a part-owner of the Lakers for several years. Johnson also is part of a group of investors that purchased the Los Angeles Dodgers in 2012 and the Los Angeles Sparks in 2014. During Johnson's ownership of both teams, the Sparks won the 2016 WNBA championship, and the Dodgers won the 2020 World Series championship. Combining his playing career*

and sports ownership career, Johnson has 10 NBA championships, five as a player and later as a minority owner of the Lakers.

From his humble days assisting his father collecting garbage, Magic Johnson accumulated a massive net worth of $600 million from earnings of $100 million as a player. He is still with the Lakers as an advisor, continuing to make his presence felt in the game. His passion for basketball and life and hunger to succeed were the fundamental ingredients that fuelled his courage, tenacity, resilience, and eventual self-actualisation.

There are many other stories of people from different careers making massive switches at various ages to live a more satisfying, meaningful life or simply following their passion into a walk of success. Any of these stories could be yours. It's all about *you, your* passion, *your* purpose, *your* future, *your* FuM©.

It takes courage, commitment, and creativity to carve out a new life. New career options are popping up every day. There has never been a more exciting time in history as far as the variety of careers is concerned. Millions of people work from home, especially after the COVID-19 pandemic. The world is one big village, and you can work anywhere you choose doing whatever you are passionate about.

If new business sales resonates with you as a path you would like to consider as the way to facilitate your FuM© journey, then flip to Appendix 1 at the back of the book. Check out the '*Helpful questions to ask yourself*'. Don't worry if some of your answers are 'No'. Look at the 'Yes' answers and think whether you can do the job bearing in mind the traits that led to my success.

Take the *Nos* and think about chipping away the bits to expose what you need to be a successful new business salesperson.

Think RE-CREATION

If Colin had asked me to complete Appendix 1 in the interview, I would not have answered them all with a *Yes*. Some of the eventual *Yes* answers would have taken time to process before I accepted their innateness in me.

> *I wanted to be Rambo.*
>
> Who do you want to be?
>
> Besides being yourself, that is.

The first decision is whether FuM© is the lifestyle you will to pursue. A lifestyle that depends on you living your life taking calculated risks to make sound investments to provide the right measure of certainty for living your sustained FuM©.

The second choice is how you intend setting yourself up with the capital to invest, which is as exciting as the prospect of eventual contented independence when you can say,

"F$CK YOU MONEY!"

We all see traits in other people that we wish we had. The funny thing is that it only takes a little effort to unlock them in ourselves if we want them enough. Rambo's relentless attitude rubbed off on me from *First Blood*.

I hate comments like:

"You're too lazy to even think of working hard."

"You don't have a creative hair on your head."

"What, you think you are a people person? Hah!"

"Don't tell me you think you can change at your age."

"You will never make it in the big wide world."

Comments like this are blurted out with malice, a scowl, and a cutting tone of voice.

Comments that are often met with this lame response from the recipient:

“Sticks and stones may break my bones, but words will never hurt me.”

What a crock of sh*t!

Words are more lethal than a bullet to the head. They can kill or leave you alive to suffer the consequences of their wounds on your mind.

Remember my mirror experience?

Give it a try. Look yourself in the eye.

See the person behind the eyes.

Love yourself—enough to get out of the rut that’s taking you into a meaningless retirement.

Love yourself—enough to give something back and make a difference in the world.

It *will* change your world.

Make the choice.

My choice

It's 2022; I am 49 years old and living in my chosen FuM©. I am not retired. I will never retire. I wake up every day with a purpose to fulfil. I am making a difference in the world and creating a living legacy. I am contentedly independent and comfortable in my skin. I am in the sweet spot of my planned life.

If I can, so can you.

I made the choice to change careers without the conscious recognition of FuM©, which had been incubating in my thoughts for many years. That choice was a natural progression into the mindset and culture. The choices never stop. I make conscious and unconscious choices every day to keep my FuM© on track. I have been making choices all the while I have been on this walk, the guard rails that ensure the safety of my walk. I would be remiss in leaving you with the thought that your walk will be easy or faultless once you have made the choice. FuM©, unlike retirement, comes with the caution of possible failure.

PART THREE

MAKING IT BIG - THE FUM© LIFECYCLE

Nogg was the father of FuM© without knowing it. His journey began when Aux introduced him to a mindset of unselfishly caring for other cave dwellers, even if they were not from his clan. He took Nogg under his wing, taught him how to hunt and withstand peer pressure and ridicule from his less empathetic clan members, including his father and siblings. Aux modelled a generosity and self-confidence that stuck with Nogg for the rest of his life. A valuable FuM© lesson that Nogg learned was to be content with what he had and not be selfish and greedy when he tried to stash food for later. Nogg's family of origin was in a rut of cave dweller poverty, destined to stay that way forever. What seemed to Nogg like the worst possible situation, losing his entire family, turned out to be the best thing for him. When he thought life with his family was all he had to look forward to, things turned for the better by meeting Aux, a friend and the best mentor he could have hoped for, with loads of positive energy to share.

When Nogg stood above the waterfall, madly stressed about his pregnant wife, all of Aux's input clicked into gear and set him off on the road to FuM©. The cycle began there and progressed with each step as he ran home to Zugg and his newborn baby. It wasn't a walk in the park for him by any means. His perseverance and tenacity held it together as he navigated life, adapting to the harsh, ever-changing environment and the extra responsibilities of providing a sustainable future for his growing family.

In the early days living in the newfound land of milk and honey, he was tempted by greed to take more food from the available supply, but then he remembered the Aux lessons to hold back and conserve for the future. He worked hard at building the sustainability of producing regular crops of fresh produce and taking care of the resources around them to bring an end to their nomadic existence. He became a forward thinker with a long-term vision that included the generosity to pass on his knowledge and abundance to his fellow cave dwellers in other clans—behaviour previously unheard of in his culture.

Retirement vs FuM©

And then came Dudd, the somewhat rebellious child who tested the boundaries of the lifecycle of Nogg's FuM© culture. He stepped into a living inheritance that no other cave child had ever had the privilege of experiencing. He had two options for his future that only he could fathom. He tested them both, first by adopting the arrogant attitude of believing he was the bee's knees and taking everything he had for granted. He was very self-centred, selfish, and short-sighted, thinking the land of milk and honey would keep giving without being taken care of as his father had taught him. He never realised how privileged he was to have Nogg patiently watching over him and guiding him into a solid FuM© mindset by his example.

The next chapter of Dudd's life after we left the story of him and Jegg in Duddville turned out differently than you would have expected, given his wild personality. After having intense conversations with Nogg about his attitude and a potential road to disaster, he settled down. Nogg told him he was in danger of undoing everything he had created for Dudd and his family to live in FuM© for the rest of their lives. Dudd adjusted his attitude and accepted the responsibility of carrying the FuM© message over to *his* children and grandchildren and warning them of the potential pitfalls.

You've heard about my epiphanies, changing lanes, working hard and playing hard, and making money on the way to FuM©. You've had a mouthful of the attributes and traits to do well in business and life. You have also heard that everybody has their unique FuM© number. Hence, making it big differs for everyone. The story you write ten years from now will differ from what you are about to read but remember, it is your story to write.

How I made it big

I made a killing in new business sales exactly to plan as I set out to do. It wasn't just a haphazard arrival at a destination. The plan, albeit unknown to me, was triggered subconsciously years before in a hotel room staring into the face of a rat who wanted my bowl of cereal as much as I did. He was totally comfortable and at home in his environment, being the rat he was. I was totally uncomfortable being the person I was and resolved to never ever share a room or my food with a rat in my life again. I had no choice, and neither did my mother, but that sh$tty predicament flipped a switch that would not have flipped if I lived in a comfortable, privileged environment where I felt entitled to everything I had. My mother and I had two options in that hotel room. To blame my father for everything and become two victims looking for something the world owed us to make up for our situation and still be waiting for it. Or to get the hell out of there as soon as possible and pull ourselves up by our bootstraps to prosper.

Notice I say prosper, not survive. That was not an option as far as we were concerned.

I had a goal to make as much money as I could as quickly as I could and not be poor. That developed into a refined plan of methodically accumulating a pile of money as quickly as possible. I found an environment that suited me as perfectly as a battlefield on a special mission suited Rambo. When Rambo eventually left the military, he never ended up on the skids or in a retirement home playing poker with some old-timers. He lived on his deceased father's horse ranch in Bowie, Arizona. He tamed wild horses and built an underground bunker full of intricate tunnels where he tried to escape the memories of his

past. John finally reached his FuM©, enjoying the simplicity of life. If you haven't seen *Rambo, Last Blood*, you should if you want to see what FuM© looked like for him.

Our adventurous lives paralleled repeatedly, applying our individual skills to pull off rescues and sales deals. The victories came thick and fast in our respective trenches. The battles were wars of attrition; Rambo eliminated his enemies, and I demolished my client's problems. We were pros at the top of our game, keeping our bosses happy.

We both made it big.

If the plan hadn't worked for me, I would have gone back to the drawing board and started over. There was no way I would not make it big and give up on my goal, still not realising it was another aspect of the building blocks of FuM©.

Muhammad Ali's Rumble in the Jungle is the perfect example of adapting to the environment, assessing the situation, and drastically changing tactics when he beat George Foreman. The report on the fight read like this:

The fight showed that Ali was capable of taking a punch and highlighted his tactical genius, changing his fighting style by adopting the rope-a-dope, instead of his former style that emphasized movement to counter his opponent.

He made it BIG!

Avoid detours

The only winners in get-rich-quick schemes are the ones who try to sell it to you or in the casinos where you lose to pre-set odds. You know the stories of the short-lived wealth of lottery winners.

You might think Bitcoin is a way to save you time in building assets to reach FuM©. Perhaps it could if you can predict the optimum time to buy and sell. Maybe you will dodge a bullet aimed at your brain.

Let's look at Investopedia for some clarity on the subject (summarised and edited by me).

Satoshi Nakamoto was the anonymous pseudonym used by the inventors of Bitcoin, who designed it to circumvent the traditional banking infrastructure for transacting after the famous financial collapse of 2008. It attracted traders willing to bet against its price changes. They used Bitcoin to store value, generate wealth, and hedge against inflation. Bitcoin's price fluctuations stem primarily from investors and traders betting on an ever-increasing price in anticipation of getting richer. The price story, however, has changed dramatically. Bitcoin began losing steam in January 2022. From an introductory price of zero in 2009, it moved to $0.9 in July 2010. Then from $1.0 in April 2011, it peaked three months later at $29.60 in June 2011. Following a sharp downturn, cryptocurrency bottomed out at $2.05 By mid-November on the back of a climb to 4.85 in May 2012. It settled at $13.50 in August 2012, with minor activity for the rest of that year.

It began 2013 at $13.28 and reached $230 in April. A decline to $68.50 followed in July that same year. After the October price of $123, it spiked to $1237.55 in December, only to drop three days later to $687.02. From there, it slumped again in 2014 to start 2015 at $315.21.

The year 2016 saw the price slowly close at over $900.

It hovered around $1,000 at the beginning of 2017 until it broke through the $2,000 barrier in mid-May.

It crashed by 80 percent in 2018—worse than the Dot-com bubble burst.

The mainstream investors, governments, economists, and scientists eventually took notice, which saw other entities developing competitive cryptocurrencies.

Bitcoin's price slid sideways in 2018 with small bursts of activity to the point where in June it surpassed the $10,000 mark, only to fall once again to $6,635.84 by mid-December 2019.

The COVID-19 pandemic shut the economy down in 2020, causing the price to burst into action again, fuelled by fear of government policies due to the effect of the shutdowns on the global economy. By November, it was trading at $19,157.16, and in December it was at $29,000.

The December 2020 high was smashed when the price climbed to a record $40,000 on January 7th, 2021 one month later. By mid-April, it was at over $60,000 when Coinbase, a cryptocurrency exchange went public. It went on to peak at $63,558 before taking a 50 percent nose-dive to $29,796 in July 2021. That was followed by another bull run taking it to $52,693 and yet another decline to close at $40,710 two weeks later. And then it rose again in November to $68,789, closing the month at $64,995. By mid-December, it had fallen to $46,164 and started fluctuating more with uncertain inflation and the detection of Omnicron, a new version of the COVID-19 virus that set the market aflutter.

Between January and June 2022, results showed Bitcoin's price continued a gradual decline, closing at $47,445 by the end of March then falling to $28,305 on May 11, which was below $30,000 for the first time since July 2021. June's crypto price plunge had it at $20,183 which took Bitcoin below $23,000 for the first time since December 2020.

Investopedia's caveat to the article reads like this:

Investing in cryptocurrencies and other Initial Coin Offerings (ICOs) is highly risky and speculative, and this article is not a recommendation by Investopedia or the writer to invest in cryptocurrencies or other ICOs. Since each individual's situation is unique, a qualified professional should always be consulted before making any financial decisions. Investopedia makes no representations or warranties as to the accuracy or timeliness of the information contained herein.

I would not consider the Bitcoin route to make it big because the fundamental foundation of FuM© investing is calculated risk.

MAKING IT BIG WITH BITCOIN - NOT

New York Post 23, May 2022 – Jeanette September reporting:

With hopes of being a homeowner by the time he turned 30, Steve Jensen decided to invest $25,000 in the crypto market in the summer of 2020. It was half of his savings, but since he couldn't afford a 10% down payment on a home in Westchester, he hoped his gamble on the blockchain would expedite the process after seeing friends cash in crypto to buy real estate.

"I knew it was a risk, but I saw so many people making money fast off crypto and thought it would be a good idea to invest," Jensen, now 30, told The Post.

Jensen, who lives in Washington Heights and works in digital advertising, allocated $15,000 of his initial investment to the cryptocurrency Cardano when the coin price was nearing $2. He watched its value rise: "It went to $3 and I almost doubled [my investment]. Then the value stayed at $2 for a few months. I held it, thinking it would just keep going up."

Turns out, he was wrong. Average young investors like Jensen went all in on crypto in the hopes of quickly making bank, cashing out and buying a home, car or business—or even retiring. It all came crashing down in this month's crypto-market bloodbath—losing nearly $2 trillion in value—with some investors losing everything.

As of press time, a Cardano share was going for 55 cents, making Jensen's investment worth about $3,000. And he's saddled with debt because he borrowed $5,000 against his credit card to invest in more Cardano before the market crashed. Now, a return on his investments seems like a lifetime away.

Jensen was left having to explain the market loss to his long-time partner, as well as park his plan of buying a car this summer.

"I didn't sleep for a couple of days," Jensen said of watching the price plummet on Cardano and Ethereum this month. "I'd wake up with insane anxiety," he added, noting that he felt "depressed" by the dismal downward turn of both currencies.

"And inflation is making cars and homes even more expensive and even harder to get," said Jensen, who has lost a total of $15,000.

"Not only do I not have profits from Cardano, but I also have more credit card debt," he said, adding that he'll have to put his home buying on pause until he can pay off his debt.

So what do I believe?

I found that new business sales made me enough money to invest wisely. And those investments were made based on calculated risk.

I never thought so when I accepted the NBS job, but business materialised with big rewards and grew exponentially as I focused all of my energy on doing exceptionally well.

The path to success begins with a passion for your job and depends on how hungry you are to prosper in life. It's not about earning millions of dollars as much as it is about making enough to have some surplus cash to invest into creating your passive income; the first step to achieving FuM©. You may already be on your way there because of your attitude towards money and making it work for you. The most important part is to cultivate the mindset of what your FuM© life will look like clear in your mind. Then you sustain it until you exit the mother ship without your spacesuit.

Doctors, lawyers, architects, entrepreneurs, website developers, personal coaches, informal traders, farmers, surfers, check-out ladies or men, business owners, pilots, and nurses; fill in the blank, all can make money and reach FuM©.

Anybody can make it big to reach FuM© because it all depends on the life you choose based on your individual needs.

Dealing drugs is a sure-fire route to making it big quickly. Somewhat risky, and there's a strong possibility that you won't live long enough to enjoy FuM©. That also depends on you avoiding some serious jail time, spending FuM© in a prison cell. The daily news broadcasts are not short of stories of people who have tried the risky route of bribery, corruption, and thievery to speed up making it big—poor choices I hope you will decline. Trust me: Ponzi schemes, counterfeiting, gambling, embezzling, computer hacking, and bank robbing are not good ideas to get to FuM©.

Whatever you do, keep it legal.

What goes around comes around

As you've learned, the essence of FuM© is a peaceful, contented life without enemies or the law coming after you. Imagine trying to live in FuM© with a mobster knocking on your door every Monday morning to collect protection money. Or having to drive around the block five times to ensure it's safe before you go into your driveway because you posted a YouTube clip of a celebrity sunbathing topless on a beach in Hawaii.

Toying with the laws of karma ends up on the wrong side of what goes around when it comes around, in jail or dead.

Elizabeth Holmes amassed a fortune. Making it big, she went from zero to hero, raising $6 million from investors, promising to revolutionise blood testing, eventually increasing her net worth to over $5 billion. Then she crashed from hero to zero when the testing system proved highly inaccurate, and they charged her with wire fraud.

Joaquin *'El Chapo'* Guzmán, Leader of the Sinaloa Cartel in Mexico, made it big until 2016 when he got arrested on multiple charges and sentenced to life imprisonment in a US state penitentiary. Guzman became the most successful drug trafficker in history, putting him on

the Forbes richest person's list. He handed over $12.6 billion to the US government after being found guilty.

Each of these people had the potential to make money, reach, and spend the rest of their life contentedly in FuM©.

'What goes around....'

Joe Wicks of the social media piece is an example of good going around and coming back. He had a unique idea to help people during the COVID-19 lockdown to stay active and healthy by following his fitness regime presented on a fifteen-minute TV workout. The success hinged on participants sticking to his eating plan, which he backed up with a series of cookbooks. Joe extended his reach by producing an app that earned him around £9 million in one week.

He engineered his success through two key factors:

Working hard on building his business

Timing his entry into an arena, he was qualified to service when the demand was at its highest.

He made it BIG.

Not only did he make it big, but Joe also used his fortune to improve the lives of others, which I will deal with in the piece on legacy.

What would your ideal life look like if you made it big?

- Where you'd live
- Your regular diet
- The clothes you'd wear
- What vacations you'd take
- Hobbies you'd try
- Projects you'd pursue

How much money would you need to satisfy this lifestyle along with your other obligations?

What if I offered you an amount of money between $10,000 and $100 million?

In a survey published on the QUARTZ website in 2020, they made some fascinating discoveries. They offered the participants substantially more money than I am offering you. The question was how much they would need to live their ideal life.

The majority would undoubtedly choose the maximum amount, one would think. That makes sense if you believe people's hunger for cash to be insatiable for fulfilling their capitalistic desires. This assumption is used to justify the perpetual hunt for economic growth. Taking the example of excessively wealthy men like Elon Musk and Jeff Bezos, it looks like they are interested in making more and more money, despite the billions they already possess. Besides, more money gives you more options, and unlimited wealth allows plenty of options.

The study, however, suggests that most respondents say they don't need unlimited amounts of cash to live their dream life. The majority opted for between $1 million and $10 million, depending on age.

One of the researchers made this statement:

"Discovering that most people's ideal lives are actually quite moderate can make it socially easier for them to behave in more aligned ways to making them happy. Which begs the question of whether money can buy happiness?"

The interesting aspect of the answer came out in the difference between 32 percent of Americans choosing the largest amount compared with 8 percent of the Chinese participants. And in a second comparison, 39 percent of Indonesians versus 8 percent of Russians choosing top dollar.

Some other surprising facts that came to light in both outcomes were:

Participants who chose the maximum amount were more likely to use some money to address social issues.

Those who chose less were only willing to assist friends and family after first taking care of themselves.

This study considered a previous one to find the correlation between wealth and happiness that found a cut-off point where more money does not buy happiness or increase life satisfaction. In the US, that cut-off amount was equivalent to an annual household income of $105,000.

Doubtless, having enough to meet the obligations of food, shelter, and basic financial security are key factors contributing to happiness. But clearly, once met, it does not take millions to maintain. Living the life of our wildest dreams does not come close to the sums of money the wealthiest people seem to need to be happy. Most of us want a comfortable existence as opposed to one of extravagance.

Making it big is different for everyone. No matter what it is, it needs to be managed because money comes and goes and there's no guarantee that when it comes, it won't go. FuM© is a sustained lifestyle.

Riches to rags

I could fill this book with sad 'Riches to Rags' stories from the daily shocks of the mighty who fall from grace, ending up in the poorhouse because of what too much money has done to them. Rock stars, film stars, and sports stars end up broke and addicted to drugs or alcohol or overdosed and dead.

Charlie Sheen, who made it big as the star of *Two and a Half Men*, revealed his HIV-positive status in 2017. His ex-girlfriend slammed him with a lawsuit for exposing her to the disease that cost him a fortune. The death-knell came when Sheen had to pay nearly $5 million in unpaid taxes.

Oscar-winning actress Kim Basinger was one of the most successful Hollywood personalities in the 1990s, starring in box office toppers like *Batman, 8 Mile,* and *The Natural*. Besides her movie fame, Basinger rose to fame through a scandalous lawsuit in the early 1990s when she pulled out of the controversial film *Boxing Helena*. The studio sued for her refusal to appear and walked away with $8.1 million, forcing her to file for bankruptcy protection. The once successful actress has unsuccessfully tried to claw her way back into the movies after making it big after making one poor decision because she thought she was bigger than the movie industry.

YOU CAN'T TOUCH THIS

I recently watched the final of a surfing competition with two young men competing to be the World Champion. They paddled back and forth on their surfboards, reading the swell to select a wave with enough energy to show off their well-honed skills. Victory depended on the best performance from a short thirty-five-minute heat. The crowd suddenly sat up to watch when one of them took a wave, egging them on to do something spectacular. The good ones ended with loud applause, whistles, and cheers.

And then, one surfer got a wave that formed the only barrel of the day for him to ride out of sight, until picking speed he exited, kicked out towards the beach, and opened his arms with palms out as if to say, *You can't touch this!* The crowd went wild, and his confidence rose ten notches. Towards the end of the thirty minutes, he got another opportunity to perform. He milked everything out of it with a long floater, surfing the crest of the wave before dropping in and launching the board out of the water into a three-sixty rotation, crushing the landing (surf slang for landing solidly back on the board) for the highest score of the day. The crowd rushed down and hoisted him on their shoulders as he hit the beach, carrying him to the winner's enclosure for the prize-giving. Standing on the top step of the podium draped in an Indonesian flag, holding his trophy in the air, the look on his face repeated:

"You can't touch this!"

All of the hours spent in the sea on a surfboard, working out in the gym and sharpening his skills were rewarded with a trophy and a pile of cash. And in this young man's case, entry into the elite world tour for 2023.

It made me think of my FuM© walk and how all my hard work, planning, and careful investments were growing while I was still working for FactSet, feeling on top of the world. It was my *Goldilocks* era.

ΔII PAUSE

Investopedia to the rescue

WHAT IS A GOLDILOCKS ECONOMY?

A Goldilocks economy is not too hot or too cold but just right—to steal a line from the popular children's story Goldilocks and the Three Bears. The term describes an ideal state for an economic system. In this perfect state, there is full employment, economic stability, and stable growth. The economy is not expanding or contracting by a large margin.

The chair wasn't too big or too small, too hard or too soft; it was just right. The porridge was perfect too, and Goldilocks (AKA Bobby) was a happy man. My hard work was paying off. I was travelling away from home for twenty days a month. I was on fire doing business with my team of passionate professionals spread across offices from Africa to the Middle East and Asia. I was riding the peak of the wave, floating like the surfer dude. My next step was to take over a new territory to add to my growing empire. I was singing MC Hammer's "U Can't Touch This" at the top of my voice.

Cold on a mission, so fall on back
Let 'em know that you're too much
And this is a beat, uh, they can't touch
Yo, I told you

You can't touch this
Why you standing there, man?

I felt untouchable! Like Akhenaten, the Egyptian pharaoh who claimed to be the god Horus incarnate. You could douse me with petrol and set me alight. I could not be destroyed.

Getting cocky – Complacency

There was a time in my university career in my first year when I underestimated the intensity of the course and overestimated my ability to cope with the workload, plus taking on two jobs, playing sport, and socialising. The shock of achieving below-average results jerked me into action to reassess my situation, refocus, and get back on track in time to complete the year with my usual excellent scores. It gave me a scare when my invincibility was running out of control.

I learned the lesson then to watch myself and keep a check on my behaviour. FuM© has the same tendency to create an attitude of cockiness towards life and the grave consequences of stumbling on the path. Ancient wisdom warns us of the three letters that can destroy our lives if we don't keep our egos in check. It feels so good to feel good about our achievements. The dopamine rush becomes a constant flood when you receive compliments and recognition. And when you're at the top of your game, there is no shortage of validation from your boss, spouse, friends, and colleagues if they are not jealous of you. The ego will fuel your arrogance and define the implications for FuM@. It is dangerous if you do not recognise it and deal with it to avoid landing at the bottom of the barrel, wondering how you got there or calling a time-out to get your ego in check and continue, finally reaching FuM©.

Jay-Z thinks he's better than De Niro

A famous rap artist making millions, married to beloved singer Beyoncé, thinks it's okay to be cocky. Not slightly cocky, Jay-Z ramps up cockiness to a whole new level.

He's not new to cockiness, as this response to being accused of a lack of social responsibility is a case in point.

"I'm offended by that because, first of all, and this is gonna sound arrogant, but my presence is charity, just who I am, just like Obama's is. Obama provides hope, whether he does anything, the hope that he provides for a nation, and outside of America, is enough."

Oh my word, Jay-Z!

More recently, he had the audacity to snub iconic actor Robert De Niro. A man who is publically a big fan of Jay's music. De Niro says he called Jay-Z six times with zero response. Not one call back! He expressed his dissatisfaction, saying, "It doesn't matter who you are. If someone calls you six times, you call them back. It doesn't matter who you are. That is just rude."

Adam Levine says, "I'm not arrogant, I'm cocky"

Adam Levine is apparently a sex symbol, but that does not give him the right to act like a jerk. Debatable! In an interview with GQ magazine, Levine commented on his public image. *"I'm not arrogant. I'm cocky. It's different. Cocky is playful."* Most people would disagree with that.

His attitude shines through as a host on *The Voice*, where he continually blows his own trumpet and is downright rude to his fellow judges. He thrives on the attention he gets as a musician too. A *Details* magazine article quoted him as saying, "I love attention. I can't stand not having it."

These people and many more like them have not come to terms with the serenity of ancient wisdom that separates their egos from their true selves. It is so sad when the external adoration disappears, leaving them alone with themselves. They often turn to substance abuse to medicate the feelings of loss and grief. As you read the rest of this piece, you will see how insidious the ego is and how important it is to separate its influence from your well-being.

> ***"Arrogance and complacency are two of the main sins for failure!"***
>
> *Futurist Jim Carroll*

The English language has some big words that mean very little and some tiny words that pack a bigger punch than Muhammad Ali. Take *floccinaucinihilipilification*, which means valueless and never gets used except as an example of a very long (twenty-nine letters) word. Compare that to the three letters of *ego*. We all know what that means. A regulated, healthy ego is an invaluable attribute critical to bolstering solid self-esteem. It is much more potent than its three letters. The problem with *ego* is the elasticity of the word!

Ego can stretch longer than *floccinaucinihilipilification* when it's inflated to become a dangerous hazard with havoc-causing potential.

The ego can swing either way when things are going according to plan. Your cockiness will cost you the plot. Arrogance and cockiness are a quick slide down a very slippery slope.

Positive self-worth is like looking at yourself from the outside and feeling proud of what you see. Not the appearance but the whole package of you. Your activities, interactions, achievements, and perception of how others see you.

Here's a scenario

You're doing well. The job's going fine, family life is good, you're feeling fit and healthy, and the future is filled with promise. Best of all, your bank balance and investments are better than expected.

You should splash out on that Lamborghini you've always dreamt of because you can afford it, and you deserve it, and your mate Don just got himself a Ferrari.

Which one is talking to you?

What is your self-worth telling you?

Which one are you going to listen to?

You decide to put it on hold.

Well done!

Remember Akhenaten, the pharaoh from a few pages back? He thought he was a god. He planned to leave a powerful legacy that was destined to last forever. He got so cocky that he tried to change the polytheistic worship of multiple gods to a monotheistic religion worshipping only Aton, the sun god. The subsequent pharaohs removed his name from the list of Egyptian pharaohs forever. They wrote him out of their history! An extreme case for sure, but close to some of the stories we hear about today.

Silence like a cancer grows

The famous line from Simon and Garfunkel's "Sound of Silence" actually shouts out a warning. The egotistical self-talk in our heads screams at us so loudly it drowns out our rational mind, and we potentially forge ahead regardless and end up saying to ourselves, *What was I thinking?* Exactly, what were you thinking? When you ask that question, it's time to go back and examine your thinking. You will discover that your ego got in the way.

A TOUGH LESSON

I asked myself the question writing on this topic and felt 1990 déjà vu when I was seventeen years old listening to the MC Hammer song "U Can't Touch This". I was feeling invincible. It resonated loudly within me because things were going well for me. I had recently graduated from high school on the honour roll at the top of my class and received a basketball award. I had a part-time job making good money and contributed to the monthly housekeeping. I paid cash for my first car. MC's words fed my inflated ego, making me feel invincible! I got cocky and made a dodgy decision to satisfy my greed for more cash. I got fired.

The most common hubristic stories come from decisions made in the military and medical circles, by excessively proud, ego-driven knuckleheads that can lead to fatal consequences. Egotistically fuelled decisions in the business world can also have dire consequences.

One such incident recorded on December 30, 2011, in the New York Times by Floyd Norris, a financial journalist, described the consequence of billionaire Eddie Lambert's cockiness. He purchased Sears Roebuck for a very low sum based on the arrogant belief that he knew more about the retail business than the seasoned Sears executive team. His flawed conclusion was that their incompetence had driven the previously successful company to impending bankruptcy. A further flawed belief was that his idea of a 'property play' purchase would produce the prospective liquidation of the company to make him a ton of money by selling off the valuable real estate owned by Sears Roebuck. Lambert, however, predicted that the company he had purchased could be profitable if he refused to imitate its competitors, who, in his estimation, were unwisely spending too much of their capital renovating their retail stores. Another flawed belief. The company executive's warnings that the retail stores badly needed refurbishing to stay abreast of the competition got them all fired and replaced by an inexperienced team, unlikely to oppose the boss's decisions: a bunch of yes-men. They predictably lost sales to their upgraded store competitors. Lambert's net worth took a massive dive, and they closed 150 stores. The backstop property play kicked into gear, leaving 300,0000 employees looking for new jobs. And this was all because of the hubris of one man who turned out to be far less brilliant than his ego and his staff told him he was.

THE LINE BETWEEN SELF-CONFIDENCE & COCKINESS IS VERY FINE

If a crowing cock has ever woken you, you will know how loud they are, and if you look out the window to shout them into silence, you will have seen how their chests stick out with pride. Arrogant birds! No different is the person at the office water dispenser loudly boasting and singing their own praises about some achievement or how they helped an old granny cross a busy street. The thing is that, just like the crowing cock, these people never stop. The line between self-confidence and arrogant cockiness is paper thin.

So is it cockiness or confidence?

Cockiness emanates from a different place to authentic self-assuredness, which is internally sourced. Arrogance comes from self-esteem based on external influences like financial standing or constant praise. The balance between healthy self-worth and egotism is upset when the external stimulus melts, taking self-worth with it.

Authentic self-confidence displays the accurate image of a person's traits and character; enough to trust themselves to show up without disguised insecurity. The authentic person learns from their failures, rather than being defined by them, progressing in life wiser than before.

A genuinely self-assured person takes responsibility for their choices, admitting their mistakes without apologizing excessively or making excuses never attempting to justify them. They accept they are just human beings that are inherently no better or worse than anyone else. They understand that life is not only about triumph; they are imperfect, fail sometimes, and have bad days.

A cocky person will pass the buck and deny guilt because they fear risking their fragile identity that might disintegrate when they fail or desperately want to avoid criticism. Arrogant people go to extremes, deflecting blame or excusing themselves for being human.

Questioning your behaviour for cockiness is a good sign that you are within the realms of good self-confidence.

People who confuse ego with self-confidence:

Listen to advice but rarely follow it

Look for flaws in others' thinking

Try to do everything themselves (entrepreneurs should not design their own websites)

See some things as being beneath them – like paying the bills

Keep ploughing on, even when they are wrong – a huge ego issue

Alienate people over time – but don't question why they've gone

Where does complacency come into the equation?

Good question.

When the line between self-confidence and arrogance is crossed, the world of delusion opens its arms and welcomes you in. It's like boiling a frog in a pot of water. If you throw the frog into boiling water, it will virtually walk or jump on water to get out. If you place a frog into a pot of cold water and slowly turn up the heat, it will get comfortable and enjoy the warmth until it is boiled alive in a state of delusion that it feels good to be warmed up.

Simply put—complacency is a false state of safety.

It's a proven fact that delusion leads to complacency in all walks of life, from politics to finance to national and individual complacency.

A prime case of arrogant complacency came to a crashing end in 2008, bankrupting the 164-year-old American banking system with Lehman Brothers' subprime mortgage scheme. The consequences of their delusional view of sustainability linked with their arrogance brought

about a global financial crisis and what was called the Great Recession. Complacency was not restricted to Lehman's either; the Federal Reserve could have averted the catastrophe had they pulled their heads out of their rear ends and decisively implemented restrictive measures.

That was certainly a mammoth consequence compared with the microcosm of our individual FuM© journeys, which can also end in disaster.

From a psychological perspective, they tell us that on the continuum of striving and reaching success, there is a point where success turns into boredom when the challenge loses its lustre. Red lights should start flashing and warning bells ringing when boredom sets in.

Even big game hunters get bored. It is an exciting activity that gets the adrenaline rushing through their veins when they see the animal in the sights of their powerful rifles, pull the trigger, and continues long after they see it drop. Ask any professional hunter how they feel after bagging their umpteenth kill. They will tell you they get bored with it. Complacency sets in, making them so cocksure of themselves that they forget that some of their prey are hunters too. Scott van Zyl is a case in point. Scott, a professional South African hunter, was hunting in Zimbabwe and ended up as crocodile fodder. It cost the lives of three large crocodiles, earmarked as suspected killers near van Zyl's last footprints to confirm. Two crocs died in vain, leaving van Zyl to be identified by DNA testing the stomach contents of the killer. Hunting solo, his complacency cost him his life.

The thrill of the hunt in new business sales got my adrenaline pumping until I saw the ink of a signature appearing on a contract. I never got bored with it and still enjoy a hunt, whatever it involves, whether it is setting up a new business, planning a vacation, or playing poker. Building my passive income has always been an exciting adventure that I continue with today.

The question in the cycle of striving for FuM© is whether you will get bored and neglect nurturing it when it is going well. The career path you choose to fund your investments is a hand-in-glove relationship to sustain the excitement of the process. I never sat back gazing at my NBS trophy cabinet, thinking I had arrived because my passive income plans were on track. I also never let my financial situation tempt me into overspending and taking for granted that there would always be more. There is, however, no way to predict this happening, so when it does, heed the warning and avoid the pool of quicksand. It only takes a toe on the edge to get sucked in.

If you're in doubt, listen to my story.

I'm making it big, very big in a great NBS job, living my dream. I am noticed in the organisation. Not just in the office where I work but globally in every office. I am on our competitor's radar. I am at the point where I call myself an expert. I generously pass my knowledge on to others. I get a call from a competitor making me an offer I can't ignore. I accept it and tender my resignation. It backfires on me, and I am out of a job. Not only a job but also restricted from working in the same industry for two years. There is no way to reverse my decision.

I act fast!

Acting quickly and making big decisions have gotten me to where I am today. I could press pause, reflect on my situation, refocus, reset, consider my options, and move forward. The bottom line: I learned from that situation and progressed. I re-aligned my thinking to gear down and speed up towards FuM©. My recovery helped me to avoid future disasters. Looking back, I am so grateful that I did not implode. The reality of the situation was that I could have and not have been able to resurrect my crushed spirit.

What did I do?

I did what I always do in tight situations.

I looked up at the night sky, saw Orion's belt, got back on track, thrived, and avoided a destructive downward dive.

Greed, arrogance, boredom, and complacency chewed me up and spat me out. I relapsed badly. My saving grace when I look back is my deep aversion to social media. I had grown out of it since my days of idol-worshipping sports stars and movie actors. It was a lightbulb moment when I saw through the smokescreen obscuring my greed, arrogance, boredom, and complacency. I took my eye off the prize. FuM© was not fully formed in my mind yet, but that incident was a significant building block.

I now see it as living life like I am making a movie, shooting the same scene repeatedly until the producer chooses which one 'goes in the can'. The bad news is there's only one take of the scenes in our life's movie. So now I ask myself the question,

"What do I want my movie to look like?"

←← **REWIND** 200,000 years

Nogg and Dudd have reached the stage where they are perfectly set up for contented FuM©. They're sure of having more than they need to live comfortably in abundant surplus for trading with the neighbours, as long as the weather plays along with good rainfalls. Careful planning, hard work, and perseverance have eventually provided an uncomplicated lifestyle.

AND THEN?

Dudd has an itch he feels he has to scratch or go crazy.

WHAT WAS THE ITCH?

He is tempted to show off his prosperity and make the neighbours envious.

What does he do?

He digs a trench from the river into a weir outside his cave. It is no ordinary little dam. He shapes the hole in the ground to form a comfortable Jacuzzi with smooth flat rocks to lounge on. He positions footrests and headrests to suit each family member's curves. When it is ready, he calls Nogg and Zugg over to present his masterpiece. Dad is not impressed, and Zugg wants to know why they have become so lazy they can't walk twenty paces to the river to relax in the *fresh water*.

→→ **FF** two days

Dudd, Jegg, and the kids have enjoyed the Jacuzzi, lazing in the water for hours on end. Until, after two days, Jegg announces that she is tired of this silly pool with its stagnant warm water. She stands up, leaves the Jacuzzi, and walks twenty paces to laze in the fresh cool river; promptly followed by the kids, leaving Dudd alone in his warm Jacuzzi.

→→ **FF** Two months

The abandoned Jacuzzi is a pool brimming with life. Dudd's eldest boy has created a fish incubator to provide easy-to-catch protein. Enough to trade with the neighbours for some of their new fermented grape juice they have accidentally discovered.

Δ **PLAY**

Boredom has driven Dudd to embark on a pointless project that fortunately never turned into a disaster, thanks to his offspring.

DMU

Dudd's Jacuzzi being so unsatisfying for Jegg and the family after only two days tells me that the point when *too much of a good thing* arises has been around for millions of years. They liked their new pond for a

while until the pleasure they derived from it turned into displeasure, even though it was enjoyable to start with. Initially, Dudd enjoyed his daily soak in the river, but he got bored and thought there was more satisfaction to be had. He became greedy for more pleasure. His thoughts turned to a more exciting way to spend his leisure time. It backfired on him, and he realised that what he had in the first place was all the satisfaction he needed, and so did the family. He narrowly survived the point of getting cocky. It still bubbled under the surface, but he avoided complacency with the help of his father, who had the cycle of FuM© well under control, understanding the dangers of greed and boredom.

ANCIENT WISDOM

"When one, abandoning greed, feels no greed for what would merit greed, greed gets shed from him—like a drop of water from a lotus leaf."
- Buddha

This kind of timeless wisdom has applied forever and will not fade into meaningless obscurity as long as humans walk the earth. The quote applied to Nogg's generation and could have changed their lives as much as it did for the people living when it was written in 623 BC and still applies today. Most humans, unfortunately, do not follow ancient, let alone modern wisdom.

Modern wisdom has come up with what they think is a brand new concept called *The Law of Diminishing Marginal Utility* (DMU). It explains an aspect of human behaviour that, as we learned from the Dudd family, has been around since caves were homes. Understanding this behaviour is priceless knowledge that will help you make better conscious decisions when you are about to fall into the trap of greed.

Investopedia, the place to find all things investment and finance-related, explains the *behaviour* of diminishing marginal utility like this:

The law of diminishing marginal utility states that all else equal, as consumption increases, the marginal utility derived from each additional unit declines. Utility is an economic term used to represent satisfaction or happiness.

And the *law* of marginal utility like this:

Marginal utility may decrease into negative utility, as it may become entirely unfavourable to consume another unit of any product. Therefore, the first unit of consumption for any product is typically the highest, with every unit of consumption to follow holding less and less utility. Consumers handle the law of diminishing marginal utility by consuming numerous quantities of numerous goods.

(Updated by Will Kenton July 17, 2021)

I have dovetailed the concept of FuM©, of which *Investopedia* is not yet aware, into a graph *they* created, to help you understand the concept of DMU.

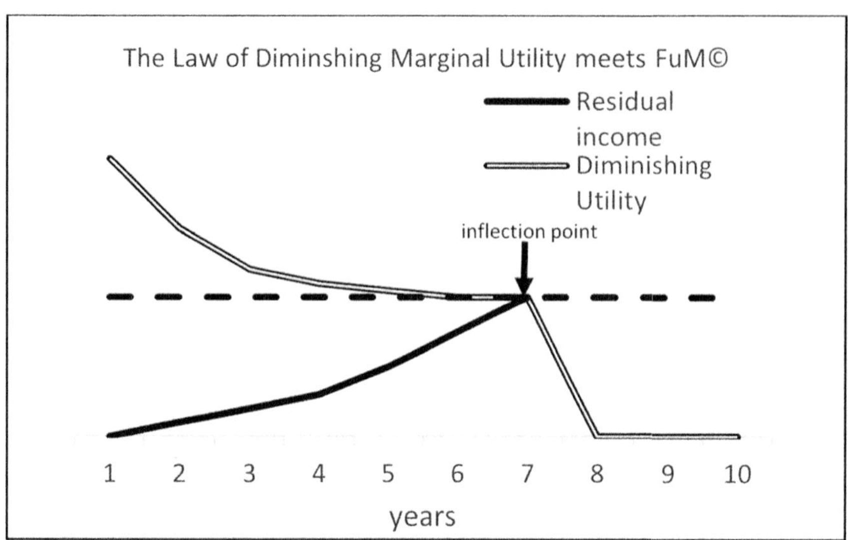

The black line is what you have been working on to reach FuM© in NBS or whatever career you choose, starting at zero and climbing with each new investment.

The hollow line is the satisfying enjoyment you derive from what you spend your hard-earned cash on, starting at 100 percent when you purchase that thing you could never afford and declining to zero with each subsequent purchase to the point where it goes into the negative the more dissatisfied you feel with the more you consume.

The broken line is the level of passive income you will use to spend your days enjoying life and having the means to sustain your unique FuM© lifestyle.

The inflexion point is where the wheels must be solidly bolted on to avoid FuM© derailment. Where greed, social media, and your environment can send you down a rabbit hole, chasing shadows, eroding the passive income you have patiently built over time.

The inflection point is the where you will spend your time, the place where the people you hang out with most of the time will play a major part in supporting or derailing your FuM© choices. The time when you have to make sure you don't get swept up in the energy of fads and impulses triggered by emotions, environment, or the dreadful social media.

DMU today was the same in Nogg's clan 200,000 years ago. This condition of the human psyche still governs us. Just ask the Jones family, celebrating Dad Jones's promotion with a meal at their favourite pizzeria.

Seven-year-old Jack, the youngest, imitates his burly teenage brother, Buzz, ordering a large pizza with extra toppings.

The first three slices taste great. The fourth is not as good but still tasty. Biting into the fifth slice, Jack is not enjoying it as much but soldiers on, keeping up with Buzz. By the sixth slice, he hates it.

"How's the pizza, Jack?"

"I feel like I could burst. It's kinda gross!"

Isn't that *just the way it is*? From the first fantastic slice, the pizza loses its value gradually slice by delicious slice, as gratification and satisfaction diminish.

Same pizza, different responses!

Fortunately, Buzz was on hand to exceed *his* DMU, which miraculously only happened after his tenth slice.

DMU is alive and well today and will live on until we expose the lie that the *fifth* slice of pizza will taste as good as the *first.*

My advice for building your passive income based on the law of DMU is to do it step by step on the four-slice rule. By the time you reach your FuM© status, you will be living every day on four delicious slices of pizza and passing the other four on to someone who will enjoy them even more than you enjoy your four.

Ancient wisdom applies directly to the FuM© culture as much as the modern wisdom of DMU.

Circling back to my pre-FuM© days working in new business sales, I have a story to tell about already living within the restraints of DMU boundaries.

I'm living in Dubai, the place I dreamt of as home for years. I have some spare cash to splash on something I want rather than need. I want to fulfil a childhood fantasy. I want to buy myself an Aston Martin.

Will the Aston Martin make me content?

Yes—for a while until another one catches my eye.

Will it make me anything more than I am?

No.

Can I afford it?

Yes, I can buy a *new one* cash like my first two cars.

I look around for a good deal on a pre-owned Aston Martin and realise my fantasy.

I loved that car and never tired of it.

The very wealthy global role model Warren Buffett drives a $50,000 Cadillac XTS. He could own a Rolls Royce Phantom, setting him back a cool $500,000. Yet Mr Buffett prefers to spend a tenth of that on his car. His level of contented satisfaction doesn't depend on the amount of money he has or the stuff he owns. Starting eighty years ago in 1941, Warren patiently built his assets from the tender age of eleven. Today, he is one of the wealthiest men in the world.

Now, eighty years later, at 91 years of age, Warren Buffett is still investing and looking for new opportunities every day.

You might think the man is greedy. I disagree; I believe he has the right mindset.

Here's the kicker, which comes from a comment he made in 2021.

"More than ninety-nine percent of my wealth will go to philanthropy during my lifetime or at death."

Asked what his secret to success is, he says it comes down to setting goals. It has changed over the years from being totally goal-driven to *Go to bed a little smarter each day.*

Adapt and Transform – Optimus Prime

Remember Joe Bloggs knitting bed socks in the retirement home? He missed the FuM© boat and the promise of an amazing retirement. He is doomed to see out the rest of his life looking like a washed-out old man surrounded by his knitting. The sad truth is that there are millions of Joe and Joanne Bloggses knitting bed socks waiting to exit the planet, blaming the world for not delivering on its promise of paradise. They live in a milieu that dishes up a daily dose of despondency that will keep them there until they die or by some stroke of luck manage to escape. Imagine Joe sipping cocktails like Bob, his school buddy, or playing golf every day like Morgan. Do you think he would even think about picking up a pair of knitting needles?

These people came from the same background, similar environments at school, and possibly at home. Joe vs Bob and Morgan. What made the difference? *Fate*? Joe probably relied on chance (whatever happens happens). Bob and Morgan took a different route, changed their situation, and transformed as they progressed. Poor Joe regressed. There's no guarantee that Bob and Morgan won't face some challenges in their future. What if Sue gets cancer or Morgan falls off a ladder and loses the use of a leg? Or Bob's parents are in the same situation as Joe with escalating medical bills they need Bob to help with?

Taking care of my wife and kids was part of my FuM© plan. I never dreamed I›d have my ageing grandmother living with us, needing 24/7 care. The unplanned medical insurance and alterations required for our house to accommodate her were unpredictable.

The cycle of life is no respecter of environmental conditions, financial status, family situations, or *FuM©* for that matter. Life happens, and we have to cope with it. The enlightenment of ancient wisdom needs to be perfectly moulded into the reality of dynamic capitalism to sensibly manage a sustainable FuM©.

Understanding Modern Capitalism

According to an article published by the International Monetary Fund (IMF) in 2015 written by Sarwat Jahan and Ahmed Saber Mahmud, capitalism was described after the opening statement as:

"Free markets may not be perfect, but they are probably the best way to organize an economy."

Capitalism is often thought of as an economic system in which private actors own and control property in accord with their interests, and demand and supply freely set prices in markets in a way that can serve the best interests of society.

The essential feature of capitalism is the motive to make a profit. As Adam Smith, the 18th-century philosopher and father of modern economics said: "It is not from the benevolence of the butcher, the brewer, or the baker that we expect our dinner, but from their regard to their own interest." Both parties to a voluntary exchange transaction have their own interest in the outcome, but neither can obtain what he or she wants without addressing what the other wants. It is this rational self-interest that can lead to economic prosperity.

A few words jump out, sounding warnings that, when taken to extremes, have the potential to cause havoc. These words are *profit, own interest, self-interest, and economic prosperity*. In and of themselves, they are good when held in balanced equilibrium. Things can tip either way as life happens during FuM©. Adjustments must be made as soon as you realise the danger of the circumstances changing your FuM© environment. Disaster can strike as quick as a wink.

A CHRIS ANGEL WANNABE

Donald Trump has a problem keeping this balance. He may not be trying to be a magical escape artist like Chris Angel, but surviving bankruptcy six times *is* pretty impressive. His greed drives him to make poor business decisions, then he bounces back to make another fortune. But who wants to live like this? Certainly nobody in FuM©. Imagine Trump being given the opportunity to make some money when he has just filed for bankruptcy. The man will never say "F$CK YOU MONEY!"

In graphical terms, our financial life is a 'J' curve starting from nothing striving to make some money and build a career until we are on the upward climb towards our goal. I wanted to make as much money as possible without thinking about how much was enough. Then I reached a point where the balance between *profit, own-interest, self-interest, economic prosperity,* and my *true self* reached a manageable equilibrium.

That's when the 'J' curve plateaued, and I knew what FuM© was all about.

Unfortunately for men like Trump, the curve looks very different. When they reach the plateau, they don't stop. Caught up in greed to satisfy their inflated egos, they keep going up the *J* until they crash. Foolishly thinking the curve is endless, not knowing when *enough is enough.* Sadly, it's at this point that many people turn to drugs and alcohol or worst of all, suicide.

Two extremes of this imbalance *could* look like this:

> Trump and his greedy, not knowing *how much is enough* buddies, living on Mars never saying "F$CK YOU MONEY!" repeatedly crashing and burning.

And

> Planet Earth, where the people combine ancient wisdom with modern capitalism, consistently saying, “F$CK YOU MONEY!” living contented, fulfilled lives.

Seriously, though, the emphasis is on the *plateau* when you reach the *number* that sustains your balance. That is why it is so important to be *100 percent* honest when you decide on the *number*. If it needs to include a Lamborghini or a beach house, make sure you factor that in. If you don’t, your ‘so-called FuM©’ will be an incomplete life of resentment and discontent.

> ***Remember: You need to adapt your mindset when life throws curve balls your way outside the realm of your pre-determined FuM©.***

ALL IS NOT LOST

Nine million years ago, a robot named Orion Pax, a defenceless dockworker, was born. His naivety landed him in trouble with Megatron, the unsavoury leader of a new group of robots. Megatron injured Orion Pax so badly he left him for dead. Fate stepped in, and someone took Pax to the ancient Autobot, Alpha Trion, who reconstructed him into the formidable warrior Optimus Prime. He has lived on for nine million years since then and recently arrived on Earth.

When Optimus Prime arrived in his robotic form, it was difficult to remain under cover and avoid detection in his quest to fight off the evil Decepticons. So Optimus Prime and his warriors, being transformers, did what only a transformer can do. They morphed into the vehicles they found on the roads. Being the leader and a very large robot, Optimus Prime eventually transformed into a massively powerful Peterbilt 4964EX tanker truck.

The new guise helped Optimus Prime infiltrate the world in an unfamiliar environment and defeat his foe. He tasted victory and lives on to tell the story. Without transforming, Optimus would have been a pile of metal in a junkyard.

"What will happen when your plateau is threatened?"

There's no guarantee that it won't be.

Will you be able to *transform* to the new FuM©?

←← REWIND 200,000 years

Nogg first transformed from living in a struggling family to living in abundance with Aux's clan. Then he regressed to living hand-to-mouth again, with Zugg almost perishing in the drought. And eventually, from hand to mouth to creating his paradise of FuM©. He dropped old habits that hadn't served him well and replaced them with sustainable forward thinking.

He succeeded with the tough job of keeping Dudd on track too, continually transforming *his* mindset to stay on the FuM© track.

Δ **PLAY**

Call it evolution or natural progression, *a rose by any other name smells as sweet*, said Juliet to Romeo. Fish evolved into land dwellers and apes to Homo erectus, then Homo sapiens. Babies evolve from birth to adulthood. It is all about change. Changing lanes is never an easy thing to cope with. A rearview mirror is much smaller than the windshield. The view of the past is just a glance that fades into the reality of the present, which is continually changing into the future.

If you want to read an excellent real-life transformation, read Andre Agassi's autobiography, *Open*. It is an honestly written, inspirational story documenting Andre's life and how he evolved and transformed

into who he is today. He learned as I did that vulnerability is not for the faint-hearted. Writing the book was a brave and cathartic experience for him, narrating his journey to find purpose in his life, after several detours. The standout for me was how he never enjoyed the game he played but subjected himself to his father's relentless domination for him to become a top-ranked tennis player. Andre's father effectively destroyed Andre the child to create the tennis star he himself wanted to be.

After he retired from the game, Andre transformed again by destroying the tennis star to become who he is today, the contented family man enjoying his wife and children. He is on the b rink of FuM©, leaving a legacy, giving back to the world with philanthropically inspired projects that are changing the lives of disadvantaged young people in America. It is a fabulous story of re-creation if ever I've read one.

My continuous transformation is now where I enjoy the exciting diversity of investment options in real estate, establishing my own companies and the relatively new untapped sources of alternative investments. Other ideas include investing in angel-funded projects and developing systems to supply scarce natural resources like water. This evolution has revived my interest in collecting art, purchasing precious metals and stones, and valuable watches. Items with increasing innate value based on demand and age. Items that are not subject to wild, unpredictable market fluctuations and uncontrollable situations like war and drought. To complete the picture, I am writing books and embarking on philanthropically centred projects to make a difference in disadvantaged people's lives. I will not stop transforming and evolving into whatever it takes to achieve anything the future needs from me.

The key to my success has been managing my investments. I focus on them, sustaining my passive income streams and adjusting where necessary, which has been top of mind throughout my transformation.

As your FuM© evolves and requires some tweaks, remember:

Not to Panic.

Optimus Prime was around long before the FuM© foundation of ancient wisdom we learned from. He, however, understood the unequivocal truth of the need for authenticity to pull off a believable transformation. When he transformed into a tanker truck, the engine, every piece of metal, every nut and bolt was an original *Peterbilt 4964EX genuine part. He could not have fooled his enemies with a smoke and mirrors trick pretending to be a Peterbilt. It would have ended badly for him. Any half-measured transformation will leave you wondering who you actually are amongst the false reflections and smoke screens. Most humans wear a mask or two to cope with what we think is lacking in our make-up.*

The culture of FuM© is a place where authentic transformation allows you to be yourself without the need to impress or project the image you believe the world expects of you. It is an essential piece of the final 'you' that will *exist smack bang in the middle of the balance between ancient wisdom and today's capitalism.*

Nogg, Rambo, and Bobby Rakhit are all *what you see is what you get* kinda guys. We are true to ourselves.

I had an epiphany of the final chips of rock falling to the floor completing my FuM© culture.

I was my true self for the first time with all of the attributes that have become me.

I am *100 percent* honest with myself and let go of the influence the world has on me, especially social media.

I am self-aware and grounded without vanity, an inflated ego or motivated by greed or craving fame.

I say no without feeling guilty or insecure and say yes to whatever supports being true to myself.

I value my close connections even more for keeping me grounded and pointing out my blind spots.

I know in my spirit what is best for Bobby Rakhit, and I trust my gut.

I let go of any negative influences and emotional baggage.

I own my own sh$t, admit my mistakes, and learn from them, never lingering on them.

I express myself with an open mind without compromising myself and my beliefs.

My true self has given me:

Satisfaction with how I live my life

Authenticity
Autonomy
Confidence
Peace

CHANGE – Are you willing?

Change is the one thing in all this beautiful universe that remains constant. The only reason the universe still exists is because it changes and adapts to the continually evolving environment. Our planet is reeling under the pressure of climate change. And for us humans, change is not always something we plan, choose, or expect. It is sometimes thrust on us, and we have to sink or swim. Whatever the reason, we must decide what to do about it. When HSBC let me go, I accepted Colin's job offer. That was my first big decision. I wasn't looking for a job in sales, so I had to ask myself some serious questions. Was I prepared to change to fit the job? Perhaps not as radically as Optimus Prime arriving on Earth. I would be *forced* into another decision if I never adapted.

When to give up new business sales and return to my comfort zone in equity research?

You can choose whatever career fits your skillset to get you to FuM©, but one thing is sure: You need to set up a contract with yourself that binds you to three non-negotiable clauses.

First, you accept that the FuM© lifecycle will require you to make changes.

Second, your FuM© goal will always run *100 percent* parallel with your career goals.

Third, you will adapt whatever it takes to keep it that way.

Think of Nogg's life. How radically he changed from arriving at Aux's clan to rounding up his sons to assist his neighbours. Whether he had a word for it or even thought about it, *Nogg changed.*

FACT
All transformation is raw, real, uncomfortable at times and can get a little messy before things fall into place.

Realistically, your job can change, you could get married, have children, and move to a new city. Without being asked for consent, you will also adapt and change.

FuM© guarantees a state of independent contentment but does not include escape clauses or immunity from facing challenges. Unpredictable conditions will pop up like surprise targets on a shooting range. They will have to be faced, dissected, understood, and dealt with. Then adjustments will need to be made to stay focused on the FuM© goal.

The good news—and there is always good news—is that not all change requires massive diversions from where you are. A one-degree shift in direction can change your destination over a 20-year journey to a different continent. What is important is to keep going forward.

Change for the sake of change is also not good. If it's not broken, don't try fixing it. Chasing fads will drive you crazy and take you off course. Assess change for feasibility and necessity before you commit to it.

I have never made changes simply for the sake of making a change. All the changes, large and small, have positively impacted my journey. The most recent have supported my FuM© and influenced what I *really* want to do.

Besides the uncertainty I faced when Colin offered me a job, I had to deal with the confusing conversation going on in my head. Arguing this way and that, telling me I was incapable, unable to sell, that I would regret taking the job, I was crazy to consider it, I shouldn't trust Colin. . . blah, blah, blah. . .

Australians call them the *Itty Bitty Shitty Committee.*

And the loudest member was screaming at me:

SELF-DOUBT!

Instead of letting self-doubt debilitate me, I chose like, Rambo, to believe in myself and accepted the job and the call to change. After taking on the challenge, rolling up my sleeves, and getting stuck into the job, I never heard from the committee again.

Charles Darwin was an example of having enough self-belief to keep the committee quiet when he put his reputation on the line by sharing his theories on evolution. He believed he was a product of evolution from Homo habilis 2.8 million years before. Everything he thought about evolution would not have been taught if he didn't shut off the loudest voice in the committee shouting SELF-DOUBT at him.

Having a cheerleader helps when the voices of SELF-DOUBT are loud and confusing.

Nogg had Aux in his corner, Rambo had Trautman, and I had Colin.

Fear and doubt are the ne'er-do-wells in the Itty Bitty Shitty Committee that proudly claim millions of victims. It takes courage, vulnerability, and honesty to own up to your shortcomings, do some changing if necessary, and shut them up.

Dust to Dust ~ Ashes to Ashes - Insignificance

Isn't it amazing how much we have learned from Nogg? Almost at the end of the book and still teaching us valuable lessons. But do we know anything about him after his story ended? Do we have any of his remains to show for his life? No bones, bearskins, rock tools, descendants...

Has anybody seen Adam or Eve around lately? The story tells us that Adam was formed from the dust of the earth. Eve was a little more sophisticated, formed from a rib bone. But we have nothing to show for the two of them either.

Then I think of men like Einstein, his good friend Marcel Grossmann, a gifted mathematician, and Michele Besso, an engineer. All three men made massive contributions in their respective fields. I admire these men immensely. They left a mark, but where are they now? Modern scientists, mathematicians, and engineers have improved their contributions and will also leave the planet.

The Kardashians, who have made a useless impact, will also depart the planet, leaving absolutely nothing of value.

When all is said and done, the notoriety, success, and fame that is heaped on people for some creates cockiness and for others just knowing they

did a good job inevitably ends, revealing our insignificance in this vast universe.

Who are we? Really...

The scene is respectfully solemn. There is an open casket beside a lectern. The unsmiling, teary-eyed mourners dressed in black have paid their last respects as they viewed the lifeless body. Now they await the final words to be spoken over the deceased, unheard by the corpse bid a final farewell.

'Ashes to ashes. Dust to dust.'

And that's it. The coffin rolls away to the crematorium for incineration. The ashes will return in an urn for the family to keep on a mantle or spread in the wind somewhere memorable. The mourners leave to enjoy tea and cake, or perhaps some stronger beverages, and chat about the person in the coffin, never again to walk on planet Earth.

A story of mortality

In ancient Roman culture, when a general returned to his town riding proudly on his horse, having tasted victory conquering another, Auriga, a slave would approach and say to him, "Remember you are mortal." This humbling notion has similar connotations to ashes to ashes, dust to dust. It reminds us we are but mortal humans with an expiry date, and that we can do nothing outside of God's will. And when our life ends, our bodies will return to the earth as dust when our bodies decay. This pride check makes us uneasy, and most people don't like to hear it. What happens to the soul is a whole other discussion, but as far as the earthly space suit is concerned, it has done its job.

Philosophy becomes reality when we measure our significance in the grand scheme of things in a universe that is almost 14 billion years old. A universe we cannot fathom the extent of, considering that it takes

seven months in a manmade spacecraft to get to Mars. That's a long drive!

Not impressed?

Try jumping on board a spacecraft leaving for Pluto 2.7 billion miles away. Prepare to arrive there ten years older than when you left. Awesome is such an inadequate word to label the enormous universe. And that's only the part of the universe we know of. What of the ones we know nothing about? And where do we fit into the 14-billion-year history?

We arrived a little late, I'd say; it's pegged at around 200,000 years ago when Homo erectus arrived in Africa. A lot of us continue the pattern of arriving late or not showing up at all. We are slow to arrive and slow to evolve.

Feeling insignificant yet?

A LESSON IN INSIGNIFICANCE

I have been interested in cosmology since I was a kid, marvelling at how gigantic the universe is. So when I saw an invitation in the local newspaper, I would not miss the opportunity to experience some of it first-hand.

It read:

The peak of the Geminids, considered to be one of the most prolific meteor showers of the year, is after dark on December 13, 2020. Join us, away from the city lights, on the night of the 13th at Al Qudra Desert to witness the Geminids Meteor Shower!

In December every year, Earth crosses the orbital path of an object called '3200 Phaethon' (such a cool name), a mysterious body sometimes referred to as a rock comet. When this happens, 3200 Phaethon sheds

debris that crashes into the Earth's upper atmosphere at around 130,000 km/h and vaporizes into the colourful Geminids meteors.

I was not going to miss this! It was estimated to take place between 22:00 and 03:00. It was with great anticipation that I took my wife, two kids, and some friends to watch the universe showing off. Armed with a powerful telescope and enough refreshments, we set off for the midnight spectacular. Oh boy! We were not disappointed. No state-of-the-art video or high-resolution photograph can compare to the live show we experienced in the desert that night.

I picked up a handful of desert sand and let it run through my fingers, grasping my insignificance in this massive universe. There was me, somewhere between the expanse of the night sky and a grain of sand.

Any egotistical arrogance in me melted into humility as I watched a performance that no human technology could recreate.

"Never forget where you came from."
Santosh Chattertgee - my grandfather

"Never forget where you came from. It will keep you humble and will keep you out of the complacency spiral."
Bobby Rakhit

When I compared reality to the philosophical outlook of this life, I discovered another brilliant facet of FuM©.

As small and insignificant as I am in this infinite universe, I can make an impact while I still have breath in my lungs.

Maybe not as spectacularly as the meteor shower or the asteroid and comets that wiped out two global populations. But I have potential. Like everyone else, no matter who, from whatever background, level of education, social standing, financial worth, religious belief, height, weight, or food preference. The fact is that there are millions of us insignificant people making a difference every day when we decide to

engage our 'significance gear' and start accelerating on a path to make an impact.

The last I heard of Nogg and Dudd, the *old man* had stopped taking himself too seriously and was trying to teach Dudd to do the same. He had first-hand experience of mortality when his family was wiped out. He knew he would close his eyes for the last time someday too. He accepted his insignificance in the land of cave dwellers and did a great job of creating a generation of decedents with strong genes, starting with Dudd. He was living a contented, independent life, remembering Aux teaching him life lessons beyond merely surviving. Making a difference came naturally to him when his neighbours needed him. His example planted a seed in Dudd's mind to have the same attitude when he finally matured.

And they lived happily ever after...... Until the end!

AN UNFORGETTABLE KNOCK ON DEATH'S DOOR

The fragility of life and my insignificance flashed through my mind as I lay writhing in pain, incapacitated and holding back tears on soft green grass. In the space of a millisecond, a projectile in the form of a six-year-old boy had crashed into my leg, dislocating the kneecap, pushing it up into the flesh of my thigh, and inflicting pain that I can imagine only childbirth could equal. With eyes so tightly shut, not even the blinding sunlight could get through the darkness behind them, and I was close to blacking out.

It was 2016, and we were on a family staycation at the Waldorf Astoria up at the Palm Jumeirah, a five-star luxury hotel forty minutes up the coast from where we live. It is a paradise for a family holiday to relax and enjoy the many activities. My two sprouts were just the right age to enjoy the Kids' Club activities, one of which is the reason for this story. It was a dad-and-son soccer match my son and I weren't going to miss out

on. It turned out to be a very, very painful lesson for me. No matter what size your opponent is, they have the potential to hurt you very badly.

The nightmare was only beginning. A hair-raising ride to the local hospital only proved that there was no competent medical support to deal with my situation. All I got out of the trip was some painkillers and another hair-raising trip back to the hotel to try and sleep the night away so my wife could drive me back home to find professional medical attention. Getting into the car the following morning was another excruciatingly painful stiff-legged manoeuvre. Only I knew the fragile margin between passing out from pain and staying conscious, suffering through it. It was the longest trip I have ever had in a vehicle that seemed to slow time down, so minutes felt like hours. I was lucky to have some connections that introduced me to the top medical surgeon who worked for one of the sheiks. It still didn't get me into immediate surgery but put my mind at ease, knowing that I could not be in better hands. There were several hoops to jump through to secure a medical facility and set a date and a few weeks of preparing me for the operation.

With all of that behind us and with one week to go to surgery, I lay unconscious on my lounge floor, having suffered a pulmonary embolism as a result of the injury, sending a blood clot from the knee into my bloodstream. I came around with two paramedics hovering over me, having resuscitated me out of a potentially fatal coma. I was transferred to a medical centre where X-rays showed how close I had been to death. The clot was arrested on its way to my heart by a bone in my throat. The knee operation was put on hold until the clot was dissolved and the threat of more clots was under control.

I was fortunate again to have a brilliant doctor on hand to save my life. He worked patiently, dissolving the clot after almost a month of treatment. Even then, I was still not out of the woods because I could not find an anaesthesiologist prepared to risk losing a patient in surgery, given the danger of more clots forming. I had to jump through more hoops with my surgeon to obtain special permission from the sheikh of another

emirate in a different jurisdiction to perform the surgery. I was not going to give up until I had to, to avoid the horrific alternative of having my leg amputated. It was a narrow five percent margin that I would make it out of the operation alive, never mind having two legs intact. A top cardiologist was brought in on stand-by to manage my well-being.

→→**FF** Four months

After major surgery, I was getting up on my crutches with help, trying to ignore the intense pain as the rehabilitation process began.

→→**FF Another fourteen months**

I walked out of DISC, the medical practice I visited regularly to nurse my knee back to strength, eighteen months after the collision that turned my entire life upside down.

→→ **FF A few years later—the saga continued**

I was climbing the stairs to a restaurant at the TAJ hotel with a bunch of mates for our annual guy's Christmas party when my other knee went out on me. It was an unprovoked patella dislocation that sent me crashing to the floor in a heap of agony, probably due to me relying on it more to reduce pressure on the injured right knee during its recovery. The repair this time, however, was easier in most respects, especially the recovery time. Nermine, my physiotherapist from the first knee, played a critical role in saga number two, getting the knee healed quicker.

→→ **FF 2022**

Both knees healed, but they will never be 100 percent again. Nevertheless, I am super grateful that I am alive. I can walk normally, cycle, and get physically fit after hearing that I would need a walking stick for the rest of my life.

In the days following the first displacement, I felt justified to ask a question that deserved an answer:

"Why me?"

Now when things go wrong, I ask myself the question that answers itself.

"Why not me? What makes me so special I should escape adversity?"

The survival of the fittest

I am by no means the only person on the planet to be interested in the universe around us. I find it fascinating to think that there could be life out there. *Why not?* My interest in the Stone Age got me thinking of the parallels between then and now. The capacity of our brains definitely differs from the cave dwellers when I consider how long they were around and how little they progressed, other than Nogg, that is. I am also interested in the anthropology of our modern era and the vast differences you still encounter in remote areas. Bushmen in the southern part of Africa live as their ancestors did, thriving in some of the most arid regions of the world. There is no doctor on call or a nurse at a clinic to hand out meds. They are self-sufficient and live off the land. It is not unusual for them to take a hunting trip that extends over a few days and covers many kilometres in scorching heat with little or no water. If one of the hunters dies on the trip, he gets left where he died. Considering the fact that they could be many kilometres from home with little food and water, it could be a relief to be one man down. Put another way, one less mouth to feed. I don't speak their language, but I am sure they have a term for *the survival of the fittest* and live by that creed.

They have come to terms with the fundamental laws like gravity, the weather, and their shortage of food that govern this universe, while in our modern world, we grapple with subjects like atomic and nuclear physics. An unbelievable contrast in the age we live in on this spiral arm at the edge of the Milky Way galaxy, where astronomers estimate there are six billion earth-like planets. What we have learned about this

planet is phenomenal, and what we continue to learn will never end, simply because of the evolutionary adaptation that happens every day. Take natural selection, for example.

Creatures living in an area protected by blending in with the natural camouflage of their surrounding environment will thrive by escaping detection by predators. Pending a change in the environment, like a forest fire destroying the trees and foliage, reducing or removing their natural camouflage. They are left exposed to easy detection and subsequent death. The subsequent increase in food supply for the predators swings the odds of long-term survival their way while numbering the days of the exposed prey to extinction.

The survival of the fittest, as we so bluntly express it.

Longevity

We meddle too easily in the natural cycle of life by consuming medication to prolong our lives and make pharmaceutical companies richer. Irrespective of whether we are nurturing a healthy body, we pump it full of supplements and artificial nutrients instead of getting ourselves optimally healthy. We do it without thinking of the consequences of weakening the gene pool. Natural selection of the human race can only happen in the remotest parts of the world, where perhaps those inhabitants will be the only ones left to keep the *lights* on when the rest of the developed world's folks are all in the ether.

The strengthening of the gene pool, natural selection, and the law of natural attrition make for interesting debates to find answers that look much further into our future than one or two generations. What about having a 200,000-year outlook for future generations? What about living in an apartment on Mars in of the Elon Musk Towers (next door to Donald Trump)?

Mufasa in *The Lion King* had it all worked out when he philosophised with Simba, the heir to his throne, saying,

"Yes, Simba, but let me explain. When we die, our bodies become the grass, and the antelope eat the grass. And so we are all connected in the great Circle of Life."

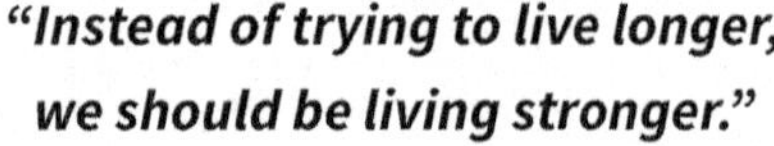

> ***"Instead of trying to live longer, we should be living stronger."***
>
> *Bobby Rakhit*

The FuM© culture is exemplified in the lion culture of Mufasa and Simba in their family structure, living in a pride. They have followed this *natural instinct* from the beginning of their existence and never changed. They function by living and working together as a team, supporting each other, unlike so many of us humans. It sounds harsh, but if we look closely at our society, we *do* apply the *survival of the fittest* regime in our *dog-eat-dog* environment. We destroy weaker individuals to get ahead.

I see FuM© as living life as the bushmen do in Africa. I just love the response from a Bushman chief when asked by an anthropologist what the purpose of his life was. Without hesitation, he said,

"To be the best bushman I can be."

The city-boy, as the chief called him, asked what he would say the purpose of *his* life was.

"To be the best city-boy you can be."

The city-boy went one step further and asked the chief if *he* left the city and come to live with the bushmen what his purpose would be. The reply came with a smile,

"To be the best bushman you can be."

A privileged experience

I watch little television, and when I do, I prefer the wildlife channels. It is where my dream came from to visit the Maasai Mara Game Reserve in Kenya. My first visit to a game park came about when I went to Kenya to meet my wife's sister and her family to garner approval for me to marry my wife. It was successful on two levels. I am married to her sister, and the Maasai Mara exceeded my expectations. The abundance and variety of wildlife in their natural habitat blew my mind. The sighting of a leopard kill topped the utter enjoyment of the visit. I can never fully explain the thrill of seeing it in the flesh with the smell of the Kenyan bush and the blood of a freshly killed gazelle in my nostrils. At that moment, I came alive with emotions I never knew existed. I became one with nature.

Being a few meters away from it was the closest experience to the circle of life I have ever had. I could not take my gaze off the panting rhythm of the leopard's body after its exhausting chase to bring the gazelle down. She kept her jaw tightly clenched around the buck's throat until its last breath and its body went limp. At which point, without leaving its grip, the leopard dragged the beast towards the shade of some nearby trees, to where our guide said he suspected her cubs were waiting for lunch.

A lightbulb moment

Nobody knows how long this planet and our species will be here. There are no accurate predictions of an impending Armageddon or any angry comets raining down on us. But looking at the two previous incidents

a few million years ago, there *is* an expiry date, we just can't find the label. Be that as it may, life goes on, and I am not about to crawl into my shell and wait for it to end. John Lennon's *Imagine*, the song people still sing every day without giving the words much thought despite the title and the lyrics. I would like to write a song called *Imagine FuM©* and have everybody thinking about it and doing it, rather than simply singing it. The first few lines would be:

Imagine the whole world living in perfect FuM©
And the planet making it for another few thousand years
After you and me become part of the ethereal energy
There will be billions of healthy people
Living meaningful, healthy, vibrant lives
Enjoying the legacy left for them to continue

It happened like this

Ping, beep, buzz, click, whatever the noise in your light bulb moment—mine was like the flick of a switch patiently waiting for me to *click*. I am so thankful for my changeable mind. It's like, *What's the good of your mind if you can't change it*?

FuM© thinking lit up my brain!

It took me by surprise, but not totally because the thoughts were locked formed in memory. When they were unlocked, my brain filled with oxygen, and I could think clearly. The world looked different. All the FuM© paradigms shifted into place, and I felt a calming flow of endorphins swimming through my veins, slowly building to the point of exuberant joy.

I've grown used to my mindset regularly adjusting as challenges come at me, along with the other 7.7 billion sojourners. The most recent adaption of living through the COVID-19 coronavirus pandemic enforced drastic changes we had to cope with. The word *lockdown* took on a whole new meaning compared to what I understood as a prison situation to isolate inmates in a secure *locked-down* facility.

When I hear or read the word lockdown now, I tense up instantly, anticipating a government announcement tightening lockdown regulations to restrict my freedom. My body receives the messages from memory, arousing old emotions from the recent past. The unprecedented global situation reshaped our thinking in a million ways from the world we knew before.

Rambo's mindset changed drastically after the colonel's speech and continued with each mission living through the pain and violence of several wars and rescues. Finally settling on the family ranch, the flashbacks continued to haunt him as he tried to find his groove again. I'm sure he had several lightbulb moments until he found it.

As for Sheriff Teasle, his mindset was that strangers threatened his peaceful existence.

Forty years ago, Marshall McLuhan coined the term *global village* in a book about technology shrinking the planet. It was called *The Gutenberg Galaxy*, and it revolutionised our perception of the world today as a big, interconnected village. Everyone understands it, but we each have a different picture of this village. I like to include the entire universe looking into the future as a universal village. And Elon Musk is hard at work trying to get to Mars and set up an alternate domicile to make that happen.

On the 24th of January, 2022, the James Webb telescope, the most powerful ever, arrived 1,5 million kilometres from Earth in its permanent cosmic corner of the universe to orbit the sun as we explore deep into the unknown, soon to become known. Despite man reaching a new frontier, I could not find one news channel reporting on it. I found tons of COVID-19 news, riots, political wrangling, and other current affairs. Everything except the historical event of the James Webb telescope.

While searching for news, I found this story that CNN considered newsworthy. A stowaway spent eleven hours in the nose wheel bay of an aircraft on a flight bound for Amsterdam from Johannesburg, South Africa, an insignificant person we will never hear of again. Compare that to the historical event of a telescope being stationed in the universe to discover new frontiers revealed by Webb's telescope, potentially life on other planets.

What does this have to do with FuM©?

Everything!

My enquiring mind took me to the point where my restricted pre-FuM© mindset was blown apart, revealing an expansive new frontier. My vision gradually cleared into sharp, clear, colourful definition from the monochrome portrait of the past. It was way beyond the confines of the previous contented well-being I had settled for. My *Webb's telescope* moment. Like folks watching *A Visit to the Seaside* in 1908, the eight-minute colour movie, for the first time. Like the evolution that has brought us virtual reality, glass-free 3D technology, artificial intelligence...

The future is an exciting place to imagine, especially if it includes FuM©.

Legacy

Remember the funeral, dust to dust, ashes to ashes?

This could have been one of the conversations over tea.

"I'll never forget what's his name, will you?"

"Never."

"Me neither."

"What was his name again?"

"Boris?"

"No, wasn't it Carl?"

"Whatever, I'll never forget him."

Some legacy!

Up to now, I've been asking you to remove words from your vocab. Now I'm asking you to make sure this one is engraved on the cornerstone of your FuM© future.

The word is *legacy.*

If words carried an impact rating, legacy would be right up there.

←← REWIND 200,000 years

Compare the possibility of Dudd and his family starving to death because Nogg carried on living Zugg's father's legacy: EXTINCTION. Nogg never left a pile of *cash* for Dudd and his descendants. He left them his wisdom and knowledge, two things his son Dudd and his siblings and the neighbouring clans could use to flourish and leave their own legacy. Cash was useless to cave dwellers, but is a great comparison with our world because cash is not a legacy. However, if you teach someone how to use it wisely, that *is a great* legacy. Leaving your descendants with the example and knowledge of the best way to do life independently content in a state of FuM©—now *that's* a worthwhile legacy.

Now you see why I want this word in your vocab, how important it is to have a future outlook rather than a single generation.

Without my *lightbulb moment* opening my vision of the future, my acceptance of a standard retirement age would not have changed. It trashed what I thought was forward-thinking and any thoughts of retirement. My legacy is unrestricted by dates and times. The *ah-hah* moment included the entire universe, 200,000 years into the future. It was more profound than discovering the *real* Bobby Rakhit. I knew what life was all about—not only my life, but the entire species.

The limited commodity of time must be spent like the precious currency that it is, giving back and making a difference. Giving yourself means that money only enters the equation when you need it for making a difference. FuM© spending forgets the old me, me, my mindset.

I asked myself,

"How can I make a positive difference in this universe?"

When the switch flipped, I 'got it'!

It was a solid fusion in my FuM© thinking.

Living in contented freedom doesn't mean I am sitting back and basking in the comfort of financial freedom to say "F$CK YOU MONEY!" to any offer of more money. I have introduced farming to my hunting skills like Nogg, to produce hundredfold yields. I spend my spare time pursuing

more than hobbies, adventures, socialising, and doing the stuff I never had the time to do pre-FuM©. I use my experience, creativity, passion, financial stability, and the desire to be generous to give back and make a difference.

I have a plan with the proceeds from the sales of this book that are going directly into the Rakhit Foundation to fund an exciting philanthropic project in Africa to uplift the lives of disadvantaged orphans through to independent adulthood and beyond, where *they* will leave legacies of their own.

The Rakhit Foundation is the beginning of a family legacy starting with me, an only child of a single mother, to hand over the baton to my children to continue the good work that I have started: *giving back* and *making a difference* in a world where negative energy often overpowers the inherent positive energy.

The spirit of The Rakhit Foundation is encapsulated in the African word 'Ubuntu', which is pronounced 'Ooboontoo'. It is a word I learned from my South African friends, that recognises the interconnectedness of humanity. In full, the Zulu phrase is *"Umuntu ngumuntu ngabantu"*, meaning *"I am because you are."* A person is a person through other people. Ubuntu originates from humanist African philosophy with the awareness that community is one of the building blocks of a healthy society. It speaks to me of compassion and humanity, the ethos of the Rakhit Foundation, to which I add humility to close the circle.

Compassion + Humanity + Humility = Healthy Community

I believe that every human walking this earth can make a difference, irrespective of whether they have any money to throw at it or not.

> ***We're here to put a dent in the universe. Otherwise, why else even be here?***
>
> *Steve Jobs*

I found a prime example of a man making a difference. Anthony Omari from Kenya is a custodian at Faraja Children's Home, run by his mother. In 2012 for two nights, three men visited them, trying to gain access to the children. Anthony repelled them by throwing a hammer, the only weapon he had, which luckily connected with one intruder.

On the third night, the three men awoke him, standing around his bed. Striking him and slashing his face with a machete, they never expected him to fight back. But fight he did, with everything he had, despite the terrible injury and being outnumbered. Anthony miraculously fought them off to protect the lives of the thirty-five traumatised children who witnessed the vicious attack. The blow to his head cut a gash from his forehead to his upper lip. It could have killed him, but Anthony survived and left the hospital within 24 hours.

Ben Hardwick, a young American student, was inspired to get involved when he read about Anthony's bravery in the news media. He raised $80,000 to support the Kenyan orphanage, travelled there, and invested his time in programs with Anthony to improve the lives of the children.

These two young men made a difference in the lives of the thirty-five homeless orphans.

It's too terrible to think what would have happened if Anthony had turned his back on the orphans in fear, complacency or disinterest. A humble man with a huge heart and open hands.

FuM© stands on several essential pillars that ensure its long-term sustainability, of which one is a legacy.

Would you like to leave a legacy?

The word brings thoughts of death, inheritance, and the eulogy delivered at your funeral. I used to think about it that way and got depressed about waiting to die to leave a legacy. There are zillions of wonderful posthumous legacy stories about loads of cash, houses, cars, jewellery and stuff bequeathed to benefactors. I prefer to hear comments about breathing humans like,

“That is such a generous person. They give me the best smile every day. It keeps me going till bedtime.”

Like Warren Buffett, I am building my legacy to make a difference while I’m alive and beyond. Writing books to change at least one life while I am still breathing. Building into my children’s lives by having a tight relationship and honest, open communication while I have the opportunity. Having experienced a few near-death experiences in my life has helped me to understand how fragile my capacity to continue breathing is.

The Rakhit Foundation is close to my heart. I am committed to ensuring its continued existence into the distant future. To ensure this, I have created strong management and legal structures that include my children with the accountability to carry the torch and multiply the influential projects and then hand the baton on to their descendants to do the same. It gets me up at 5:00 a.m. to start my day and pour my positive energy into the world around me.

That wonderful day in the Maasai Mara, seeing the leopard dragging her kill off to feed her cubs, marked a point in my life that has stayed indelibly etched in my memory. It reminds me to appreciate and nurture the culture of keeping strong family relationships as part of my legacy.

I also travel to Kenya now on business and to visit my family. When I have free time, I walk the markets among the informal traders. I look at the hustle and bustle and what looks like chaos, and I wonder what

these traders would answer if I asked them to tell me their level of contented independence.

The average yearly income in Kenya is 830,170 KES, equivalent to $19 a day. That's not a lot of money in anyone's books. The point is this I don't believe they are trying to get rich. There are no disgruntled people in those markets. On the contrary, there's laughter and comradery between traders and customers. It's a positive, contagious vibe. I always leave feeling better than when I got there.

I notice a lot of children working with their parents, setting up stalls early morning as they prepare for the day. When I am there later in the day, the children are back attending to customers. They are being mentored into the job to start their own stalls or take over when the parents are too old to count change. The parents, like Nogg, are investing in their children to sustain their FuM© when *they* can sit back and do what makes them content. It's a great picture of life in Africa. Entrepreneurs doing what they know best and passing the baton on to the next generation.

I smiled to myself watching *No Time to Die*, the latest James Bond movie when Lyutsifer Safin, the villain, says,

"Life is all about leaving something behind, isn't it?"

Even the baddies in the world know that they leave a mark!

Seriously, though, many individuals spread their wealth far and wide into projects and charities to ensure their memory on a plaque or a street name. Only they know their motives for doing this, whether it comes from their heart or a cold, calculated tax write-off.

> ***"Whatever drove them, there is another point to giving back to humankind that is far more important than money. It is our time, our knowledge, our mentorship, our energy that will ensure that the human DNA gets stronger as we give back. That's what legacy is all about."***
>
> *Bobby Rakhit 2022*

I am sad to say that the life expectancy of family offices and inherited family fortunes do not always make it through many generations. Like laying to rest the human body, they suffer the same fate of *dust to dust*. That is why it is crucial in the FuM© culture to mentor the next generation to continue to build and sustain the life of the legacy we leave behind.

> ***"Of everything we have at our disposal in this universe where we are so insignificant, our impact cannot be more amplified than by adding the essential ingredient of love."***
>
> *Bobby Rakhit*

That's the way it is

Reaching FuM© is being satisfied with the fourth piece of pizza and avoiding the temptation to tuck into the fifth and sixth pieces. It is a beautiful place to be, so different from how the world works. Unfortunately, it will not happen without radical changes in global thinking. That's just the way it is. Too many people simply accept the age-old expression and do nothing about it, as 2Pac raps in his famous song "Changes."

Come on, come on
That's just the way it is
Things will never be the same
That's just the way it is
Aww, yeah
I see no changes, all I see is racist faces
Misplaced hate makes disgrace to races
We under, I wonder what it takes to make this
One better place, let's erase the wasted

So that's just the way it is in this world, 2Pac; you say *nothing changes* even if someone tries to make changes. 2Pac lived for a short twenty-five years in a world experiencing situations that dealt with deep-seated hurt, uncertainty, injustice, hatred and false benevolence. He heard positive words from people and minimal action to bring about positive change. Nothing stuck, and he decided *that's the way it is.*

FuM© Demystified

FuM© rebels against the machine. The machine that cuts people into neat little cook-cutter shapes. Shapes created by social media, false advertising, and empty promises. By institutions that don't believe *themselves*. All the while, turning a blind eye to the consequences, consistently continuing their journey of numbed complacency.

Think banks, governments, retirement funds... who say:

"Ask no questions. Conform to the way of the world. Life will be fine."

I feel an extreme sense of urgency for change in the way the world thinks when I look at the results of the resistance to change and face up to the chaos. I compared the state pensions of the US, UK, France, Germany, and Australia to see the extent of the chaos and felt more concerned when I looked at the picture.

The eligible age for drawing a state pension varies between 62 and 65.

All of them, except France, are being raised because of a general increase in life expectancy. The age of 67 in the UK and Germany. Australia adds six months onto 66. And between 67 and 70 in the US.

Comparing the monthly pension pay-out to the working wage these people earned before retiring also sounded alarm bells. France and Germany lead the pack with 50 percent. The US weighs in at 49 percent. Australia is at 43 percent. And the UK is at a dismal 29 percent, or 63 percent, depending on the scheme selected.

Most significant in the findings is the result of projecting the outcome of complacency to take corrective action onto the number of pensioners in each respective population. It is frightening to see that,

Of the 67.6 million in the UK, 12.4 million are pensioners–18.3 percent.

Of the 65.5 million French, 14.7 million are pensioners–22.4 percent.

Of the 84.3 million Germans, 28.5 million are pensioners–33.8 percent.

Of the 26 million Australians, 4.6 million are pensioners–17.7 percent.

Of the 332.4 million Americans, 46.33 million pensioners–13.9 percent.

So, from just five countries in the world, 17.7 to 33.8 percent of their population are pensioners.

That amounts to 106.53 million people who could be in FuM© independence and making a difference in society. Instead, we have a handful of philanthropists like the Hungarian-born billionaire Hedge Fund guru George Soros. In an extract from a CNN news report, Soros commented on the 2022 war in Ukraine, saying,

"Even when the fighting stops, as it eventually must, the situation will never revert to where it was before," warned the 91-year-old Soros.

"Other issues that concern all of humanity—fighting pandemics and climate change, avoiding nuclear war, maintaining global institutions, have had to take a back seat to that struggle. That's why I say civilization may not survive."

The former hedge fund manager, who is chair of Soros Fund Management LLC and founder of the Open Society Foundations, is famous for using his wealth to help foster open societies and create inclusive democracies with governments that are held accountable.

But after the events of September 11, he noted, the tide began to turn against open societies. As a result, "repressive regimes are now in the

ascendance and open societies are under siege," he said Tuesday. "Today, China and Russia present the greatest threat to open society."

By Jeanne Sahadi, CNN Business
Updated May 24, 2022

When it comes to money and having lots of it, we live in a world of extremes where people differ as far as the East is from the West. Two super generous men, Warren Buffett and George Soros, share their wealth for good. I will leave it up to you to research some of the recent notoriously wealthy individuals and share some posthumous ones.

In stark contrast, there's the story of John Paul Getty, who had a pay phone installed in his mansion of a home so family and friends could not make long-distance calls at his expense. And if you think that sounds weird, what about refusing to pay a ransom when they kidnapped his grandson? It doesn't end there. He loaned his son the money to pay the ransom to get his grandson back and charged him interest on the loan. Getty was worth $2 billion when he died.

Leona Helmsley took things to the extreme. She was a New York hotel baroness, AKA the Queen of Mean. At one point in her life, she was being sued by eight separate contractors who had done work on her mansion and refused to pay. Her mean streak cost her eighteen months in the slammer for tax evasion. When she died in 2007, she left $12 million to her dog. Having too much money can desensitise and alienate people or trigger their generosity, sometimes disguised as tax relief, into changing the world.

We need 106.53 million pensioners to push 'REWIND' and create an FuM© culture to make a difference in society.

Sure, I know that cannot happen, but what if the current population of pre-pensioners began an Optimus Prime transformation to create their FuM©? If we start today, it will take a generation of FuM©ers before we create the potential for the next generation to continue the FuM©

culture without the burden of the present generation dragging them back. And then followed by the next generation and the next and ... and ... so on.

This paragraph is so important that I should repeat it, but I rather suggest you read it again, and perhaps again.

Picture a world of contented philanthropists doing what they enjoy every day while they change the world for the better.

Then we could confidently say,

That's just the way it is!

From evolution to revolution

Right on the heels of the American Revolution that ended in 1784 came the time at the end of the 1700s when France, which had established itself as one of the wealthiest and most powerful European countries, suffered the same fate as the USA. The fact that the poorest French classes never tasted the benefits of this wealth started the consequences of brewing dissatisfaction, escalating into an unavoidable catastrophe. As much as the powers in force could have wished to maintain a steady status quo, it could not hold. The Revolution erupted after a few short years and progressed to smother any hope of survival for the fragile regime that the upper class had enjoyed up to that point. The Revolution resulted in the deaths of King Louis XVI and his wife, Marie Antoinette, the queen who'd shown her disregard and oblivious disdain for the plight of the poor with her famous *cake* statement when she suggested to Louis that to appease the dire food crisis he should

"Let them eat cake."

It is no different today with the financial institutions that citizens rely on for a secure retirement. The parallel between the queen's outright disdain with her *cake* remark and the financial service providers today is frighteningly stark. They conveniently turn a blind eye and spend a few more million advertising to lure prospective clients into pension poverty at the legal retirement age.

King Louis created a hierarchical estate system with the monarchy naturally at the supreme level, followed by the revered clergy, then the loyal nobility and last, the masses, the bourgeoisie; the citizens. They grouped people into castes based on wealth and power, which meant the poor had virtually no rights. They were even required to pay back half of their meagre wage in income tax.

The bourgeoisie's festering anger and resentment toward the monarchy, clergy and nobility should not have surprised them.

Imagine if the 106.53 million pensioners in the world stood up against the empty promise makers.

The French king practised absolutism (sound familiar?), exerting complete dominance over ninety percent of the population. He looked after the remaining ten percent, who served him loyally for obvious reasons, and shared his *cake* with them.

His mismanagement of the country, taking care of himself and his loyal subjects, led to dwindling food supplies and the bourgeoisie living in abject poverty. The situation reached a boiling point when things erupted into a full-blown revolt. Beginning on May 5th 1789, it lasted for ten years, six months and four days, and ended on November 9th, 1799.

I believe that history repeats itself. The *powers that be* still want to control our future while they feather their own nests with our fluffy duck down (CASH). It is time to begin a revolution against greed, corruption, and false retirement forecasts to expose the systems that keep us trapped in financial absolutism. They cannot dictate how we live the best years of our life.

There is much more to FuM© than making the choice. There must be hundreds of questions running around your mind right now. That's great! You have just completed the hors d›oeuvres; the next course is in preparation. It is a dish that will provide your appetite with the expected satisfaction. The F$CK YOU MONEY series will demystify the complexity of an elementary new culture. The evolution is a continuous fleshing out of the way to optimise FuM©. Take France's years of evolution to where it is today after the Revolution. They are the fifth largest economy in the world, providing around one-fifth of the European Union›s GDP.

They are still evolving.

Where would they have been without the revolution?

Where will we be without a revolution?

The revolution to begin your evolution begins here.

The French learned from their mistakes, leading the way for many European countries. Robert Schuman was a French politician, prime minister, foreign minister, and eventually president of the European Parliament. His life bears testimony to the possibility of national transformation for the well-being of its citizens.

In all honesty, the difference we face in the world is that most citizens have options to choose how they live life, especially their future. We can choose a career, where we will live in this global village, how much we will consume, and how to spend our time, now and in our later years. The pressing problem we face in all of this is the external pressure on us when we make those decisions. The intense onslaught of social media is forming a global culture of greed and power. The unrealistic capitalist ideals dictate the need to compete in an impossible competition. Keeping up with the Joneses in an endlessly spinning hamster wheel is killing us. Like the child of an over-zealous mother alongside a sports field screaming at her child to do whatever it takes to win, we try to outrun and stay ahead of whatever we have to outrun, no matter the cost. The goalposts move every second, drawing us into the same power struggle faced by billionaires, conglomerates, and governments waging greedy battles to gain power and dominate.

FACT

There are twenty-seven live conflicts (wars) going on between countries right now. This fact, published by the Council on Foreign Relations Global Conflict Tracker, is categorised into three groups of conflict intensity:

- Worsening
- Unchanging
- Improving

At the time of writing, there is not one entry under the 'Improving' conflict group. The tragic truth they note is that conflict and violence are on the rise. This is according to the United Nations (UN). Of the world's 7.97 billion citizens, 2 billion are in areas affected by conflict. A massive one-quarter of the current human race is somewhere where governments cannot cooperate and live in peace and harmony. Shocking!

Dominance through power and money feed the limitless human condition of greed.

King Louis XVI and Marie Antoinette were not the only greedy monarchies in history and are not the greediest that ever lived, either. It appears that monarchies over time have had some serious competition when it comes to botching up their realms with greed-induced incompetence driving some of them insane. Nebuchadnezzar II of Babylon 604–562 BC began the royal trend of greedy insanity. Caligula, Emperor of Rome 12–41 AD, attempted to appoint his steed, Incitatus, to the high office of consul. Ivan the Terrible 1533–1584 lived up to his name and almost bankrupted his empire. Mary Queen of Scots, 1542–1587, was unfortunate enough to have to ward off Edward VI, King of England, and Henry III, King of France from their greedy plots for her throne. Then along came King Louis XVI on June 11, 1775 with a bunch more not mentioned, leaving a trail of dysfunctional rule in their wake.

→→ **FF** 2022

It's just another day in paradise.

Is it?

Most citizens go about daily life, never stopping to think about the universe, where it came from, why it is here, and how long it will last.

Although some of us do.

Mostly, though, it looks like people are satisfied to leave it to Albert Einstein, Isaac Newton, Charles Darwin, and my favourite, Stephen Hawking, to puzzle things out and pay them little mind. Until we hear bad news, that is, like, *A meteor is on its way to wipe us out like the dinos and cave dwellers were*. There's no Nogg to tell us what he heard or saw, so we have to listen to the experts who make predictions based on facts they unearth.

Do people today even consider themselves an individual among the 87 million that exist? Or do they assume they are something indestructibly special that will not be destroyed?

Or will we?

More to the point, it looks like we will wipe ourselves out before the meteors get here.

Humanity May Have Less Than 600 Years to Leave Earth

By Mike Wall, published November 07, 2017

Earth may be uninhabitable just a few centuries from now, so humanity should prepare to spread out into the cosmos, Stephen Hawking has advised.

"If humanity doesn't become a truly spacefaring species in the next five centuries or so, we may well go extinct." Stephen Hawking said, according

to media reports. During a video presentation Sunday (November 5) at the Tencent Web Summit in Beijing, the famed cosmologist warned that the ever-rising human population, and its mounting energy needs, could render Earth uninhabitable by the year 2600.

Hawking advised that we get our act together and boldly go where no one has gone before, *The Sun* reported. During his talk, Hawking also highlighted the exploration potential of Breakthrough Starshot, a $100 million project that aims to develop tiny, uncrewed, sail-equipped probes that will be accelerated to 20 percent the speed of light by powerful lasers.

Such nanocraft could get to Mars in less than an hour and theoretically fly by the closest exoplanet to Earth; the possibly habitable Proxima b, which lies about 4.2 light years from us, after a space journey of just 20 years, Hawking and other Starshot team members have said.

"Maybe if all goes well, sometime a little after the middle of the century, we'll have our first picture of another planet that may be life-bearing orbiting the nearest star," breakthrough Starshot Executive Director Pete Worden, the former head of NASA's Ames Research Centre, said at the summit in Beijing.

In another article from Futurism on November 6, 2017, Dom Galeon wrote about Hawking's fear of artificial intelligence (AI) replacing humans altogether, saying that it was not long before humans will be forced to flee the planet and become a multi-planetary species because we have reached *the point of no return*. This warning stems from his concern about overpopulation and the real threat of AI potentially becoming super intelligent enough to replace humankind.

In his own words:

"The genie is out of the bottle. I fear AI may replace humans altogether."

He was so convinced on this matter that he suggested the formation of a world government to control the development of the technology to protect middle-class jobs and ensure its use was banned in any form of military technology. These warnings seem to have been ignored up to now.

On the CNBC website in an article published on May 5, 2017, Arjun Kharpal quoted Stephen Hawking verbatim on the danger to earth within the next thousand years, saying,

"By that time, we should have spread out into space and to other stars, so a disaster on Earth would not mean the end of the human race. However, we will not establish self-sustaining colonies in space for at least the next hundred years, so we have to be very careful in this period."

In the same article, Kharpal mentions that billionaires SpaceX founder Elon Musk and Jack Ma of Alibaba both share Hawking's opinions. The interesting point here is that these two men are at the cusp of technological advancement.

> ***"Remember to look up at the stars and not down at your feet. Try to make sense of what you see and wonder about what makes the universe exist. Be curious. And however difficult life may seem, there is always something you can do and succeed at."***
>
> *Stephen Hawking*

It comes down to the fact that we need to change our consumer attitude towards our planet and stop destroying it. Just like we need to change our attitude toward the well-being of future generations.

IMMEASURABLE LEGACY

These brilliant scientists didn't do all of the research for themselves either. Sure, they were inquisitive and wanted to understand the

universe they found themselves in. The discoveries they made satisfied their intellectual appetites. But the immense legacy they left us was their unselfish gift of enlightening us mere mortals with the magnificent wonders of science and most importantly, warning us of the mortality of the species. They believed we could exist for many more years than the current consumption of 1.75 worlds we are consuming predicts.

Simply put, we consume much more than nature can provide.

Despite their warnings, nothing changes because like King Louis, the *world* thinks they are invincible and prefer to live in denial.

Action

We don't have to leave it up to someone else. Especially not the government!

We can make changes. We can strengthen the gene pool. We can consume less. We can explore space. We can .... We can .... We can!

Much more urgency is needed. We must .... We must .... We must ....

We have no option!

FuM© is the inflexion point where greed, freedom, and legacy exist in perfect harmony.

FuM© has the potential of producing a better testimony than the post-revolution French legacy to ensure the sustained well-being of future generations of citizens living in a culture created by the healthy union of ancient wisdom and modern capitalism. It is the closest you will ever get to fulfilling the meaning of your life.

See you there.

You can find out more about FuM© at www.fkyoumoney.org

Appendix I

Some helpful questions to ponder as you get to know more about NBS

Do you understand the difference between new and existing business?

Yes __________

No __________

Do you have a vision for your future?

Yes __________

No __________

Do you have an entrepreneurial spirit?

Yes __________

No __________

Can you take risks?

Yes __________

No __________

Can you be brutal in making decisions and carrying them out?

Yes __________

No __________

Are you a creative thinker?

Yes __________

No __________

Can you deal with rejection?

Yes __________

No __________

Are you hungry to succeed?

Yes __________

No __________

Are you prepared to fail sometimes?

Yes __________

No __________

Can you take some hard knocks and get up and go forward?

Yes __________

No __________

fkyoumoney.org

Printed in Great Britain
by Amazon